Edexcel GCSE
Citizenship Studies
Short Course
Teacher Guide

Anthony Batchelor • Sharon Shelley

A PEARSON COMPANY

Published by Pearson Education Limited, a company incorporated in England and Wales, having its registered office at Edinburgh Gate, Harlow, Essex, CM20 2JE. Registered company number: 872828

Edexcel is a registered trade mark of Edexcel Limited

Text © Pearson Education Limited 2009

First published 2009

14

10 9 8 7 6

British Library Cataloguing in Publication Data

A catalogue record for this book is available from the British Library

ISBN 978 1 846905 36 0

Designed by Steve Moulds

Printed by Ashford Colour Press Ltd., Gosport

Websites

The websites used in this book were correct and up to date at the time of publication. It is essential for tutors to preview each website before using it in class so as to ensure that the URL is still accurate, relevant and appropriate. We suggest that tutors bookmark useful websites and consider enabling students to access them through the school/college intranet.

Disclaimer

This material has been published on behalf of Edexcel and offers high-quality support for the delivery of Edexcel qualifications.

This does not mean that the material is essential to achieve any Edexcel qualification, nor does it mean that it is the only suitable material available to support any Edexcel qualification. Edexcel material will not be used verbatim in setting any Edexcel examination or assessment. Any resource lists produced by Edexcel shall include this and other appropriate resources.

Copies of official specifications for all Edexcel qualifications may be found on the Edexcel website: www.edexcel.com

CITIZENSHIP STUDIES

CITIZENSHIP STUDIES

Unit 2: Participation in Society

Welcome to the Edexcel GCSE Citizenship Short Course Teacher Guide

About this Teacher Guide

This **Teacher Guide** and **CD-ROM** have been written to fully support the GCSE Citizenship Short Course specification from September 2009, giving you everything you need to deliver this course successfully. It shows how all the resources in the Edexcel GCSE Citizenship Short Course suite fit together and gives guidance on how to plan for and implement the Citizenship specification.

The **Teacher Guide** comprises 49 sets of Teacher notes covering Units 1 and 2 in the Student Book. Unit 1 is divided into three themes. Each theme comprises several chapters which are divided into double-page spreads. Every spread in the Student Book is paired with a set of Teacher notes in the Teacher Guide which:

- point out *Lesson objectives*, linked to the *Objectives* in the Student Book.
- specify a *Focus* for teaching the spread and highlight key ideas and areas students may find difficult.
- reference *Key terms* from the Student Book.
- link the spread to applicable *Activity sheets* available on the Resource Browser.
- provide suggested lesson starter, development and plenary activities.
- provide answers and guidance to all the questions in the Student Book.

There is also an *Introduction to Unit 2*, which provides examiner's advice, key features and information on how Unit 2 will be assessed.

The **CD-ROM** includes all material in the Teacher Guide and as well as activity sheets, schemes of work, ResultsPlus and ExamZone interactive activities and more. All the Word documents are editable so you have complete flexibility to make the resources work to your specific needs.

Using the GCSE Citizenship Short Course Teacher Guide

When using the GCSE Citizenship Short Course Teacher Guide, it would be useful to keep the following in mind:

- The Teacher notes emphasise the learning objectives and topics that sometimes cause difficulties for Citizenship students.
- Additional material on the CD-ROM provides you further assistance in creating your lesson plans and helping your students.
- As events and developments occur, always try to update your material to embrace issues in the news.
- In every lesson remind your students of the three *Key Concepts for Citizenship* which they first met in the Student Book Introduction – *All about You*: Identities and diversity, Rights and responsibilities and Democracy and justice.
- Try to get students to think about how these key concepts aid understanding in each spread.

A changing and diverse society: Rights and responsibilities for all

Lesson objectives	Specification link: Unit 1, Theme 1

By the end of this spread the student should:

- be able to recognise the balance between rights and responsibilities
- understand about the different types of rights and responsibilities (human, legal, moral, political, social and civil)

Focus

Make sure students clearly understand the difference between human rights and legal rights, which they often find difficult. Also make sure they understand that one person enjoying their rights often depends on someone else living up to their responsibilities.

Key terms

- civil partnership
- civil rights
- trade union

- human rights
- moral (or ethical) responsibilities
- Universal Declaration of Human Rights

Linked activity sheets

- Who do I trust?
- Big Brother is watching you!
- Heart transplant
- Launch your own pressure group

Starter	Discuss the images in *What's the issue?*, asking students what rights are being shown. Then discuss the responsibilities that are linked with those rights. Why is it important that people understand these responsibilities? What would happen if people failed to act responsibly?
Development	Introduce each of the different rights we have and ask students to give new examples of entitled 'rights'. Start with human and moral rights, contrasting these with political or civil rights. Ask students why they think it's important that these rights become legal rights.
	Once you have discussed examples of all of these, ask students, possibly in groups, to give examples of responsibilities that are linked to these rights, in a column next to the 'rights' list, e.g:

Rights	Responsibilities
Legal right: to marry when you are 16, with parents' consent	*To be faithful to your husband or wife*

Now move on to the *ebay* activity, reminding students to think about what they have learned so far. In discussion, use the idea of empathy – *'how would you feel if...?'*

	You may wish to introduce the *ResultsPlus* feature, pointing out to students how to use the feature to ensure that they achieve the best possible marks in their examination.
Plenary	Ensure students understand the points in the *Checklist* and the key terms they have encountered.
	For homework, students could consider the *Further issues* questions or, in preparation for the next lesson, find out what the freedoms of speech, movement, opinion and privacy are about and why they are important.

Answers to questions in the Student Book

What's the issue?

Do marriages or civil partnership ceremonies involve legal or moral obligations or both?
- Marriages occur between a man and a woman. Civil partnership ceremonies occur between two men or two women. However, many people dispute whether these terms are correct.
- They involve both legal and moral obligations and consequences.
- Husbands and wives have legal responsibilities to each other and for their children. The law gives a married couple rights they did not enjoy as individuals, e.g. not paying inheritance tax if one dies.
- Morally, couples are expected to be faithful to each other and to respect each other.

Once teachers have qualified, they have the right to teach. Is this a human right, a legal right or a moral right? What are the teacher's legal and moral responsibilities?
- In the UK a teacher who has the qualifications required by the government can apply for jobs in schools or colleges. Such a right is not in the declarations of human rights but teachers are human beings, so the right to teach could be seen as a human right.
- Having qualifications does not guarantee a teacher a job, though most do.
- Once a teacher is appointed to a post in a school or college, she or he will sign a contract with the employer which sets out legal requirements such as duties, holiday entitlements and pay. Teachers must obey the laws relating to teaching. They are generally considered to be acting *in loco parentis* – in the place of parents – while children are in their care. This means they have a legal responsibility.
- Teachers have a moral or ethical and legal responsibility to look out for the overall welfare of the child, even in ways beyond their own immediate responsibility, e.g. if a child is being abused by parents or others or if a child is being made to obtain paid employment beyond the limits set by the laws in the area where they live.

Margin questions

In what ways are the responsibilities of doctors the same as those of teachers?
- Both are professionals with ethical codes for them to follow. Both doctors and teachers are regulated by the General Teaching Council or the General Medical Council as well as by employers and families.
- When a teacher takes children on a school trip, she or he has to ensure that risks have been assessed and the children will be kept safe and out of danger. Doctors similarly consider risks and dangers when deciding how to treat a sick child, including what risks there could be in prescribing medication or treatment.
- In designing lessons, teachers must teach the national curriculum and not stray far beyond the school's agreed schemes of work or raise issues that may worry, frighten or indoctrinate children.
- Doctors and teachers must consider children's welfare and obey laws that define relationships between adults and children.
- Teachers don't physically examine children as doctors do – all doctors have taken an oath to do everything they can to preserve the life and health of the child.
- Teachers would not expect to take the actions a doctor takes because their roles are very different. Some would say that if doctors are responsible for physical health and development, teachers are responsible for developing knowledge, understanding and an ability to participate self-confidently as an adult and a citizen in society.

CITIZENSHIP STUDIES

If you see someone in trouble, it is morally wrong to ignore them, though getting involved might be dangerous. How can you protect yourself and help others?

- The parable of the Good Samaritan suggests that none of us should 'pass by on the other side' if we encounter someone in difficulty.
- If we were out with friends and one of them was attacked, we would help them, even if it was a personal risk. We'd need to assess the risk and whether we could make a difference.
- If we hope that someone would help us in a similar situation, then natural **empathy** should make us want to help the person in trouble.
- If we see someone being attacked by others, we may face the dilemma of putting ourselves in danger or leaving the thugs to carry on attacking their victim.
- Even if we do not directly intervene, we can help by calling the police, ambulance or, if appropriate, the fire brigade, whose services can stop the attack, treat the injured and make the area safe.
- Sometimes we may be aware of the need for humanitarian aid following an earthquake or flood or cyclone. Many people are ready to give generously to help alleviate the suffering of people affected in the UK or overseas. It could be considered morally wrong to ignore these people who are suffering.

Think about the rights of buyers and sellers on ebay and what obligations and responsibilities they have. Which do you think is more important, the rights or the responsibilities?

- Buyers expect that the goods being sold will be as described, that the person selling them really is the owner and that once the money has been paid, the goods will arrive in good condition.
- Describing fairly, only selling goods which are your own property and despatching promptly are the responsibilities of the seller.
- It isn't a question of whether rights are more or less important than responsibilities – both buyer and seller depend on the other acting in good faith.
- Buyers and sellers have certain rights, should they need these, but also responsibilities, which they will be aware of from ebay. If the buyer and seller both exercise responsibility then neither need to exercise rights.

Review and research

Why might some countries ignore human rights in their laws?

- In the UK, 'rights' are an important part of our culture and values.
- Although the UN adopted the Universal Declaration of Human Rights in 1948 (and over 180 countries have now signed up to it), such rights are a relatively new idea in many parts of the world. In some countries religion remains all-powerful; elsewhere, 'strong' rulers (as in China) want to plan what they see as good for their country – roads, railways, towns, power station, factories and trade – without worrying too much about human rights.
- In many Middle Eastern countries (e.g. Saudi Arabia, Egypt and Dubai) such rights and other ideas we take for granted (such as democracy) are not part of the culture, so are not yet given high priority.
- How seriously different countries take human rights, and how far they incorporate them into their legal system, depends on the balance between tradition, religion, culture and political leadership in the country. Thanks to the UN Universal Declaration, substantial progress (in some places faster than others) towards human rights is being achieved in many countries.
- Lots of people in countries like the UK have fought for their rights and freedoms. Battles like earning votes for women in the UK or black civil rights in the US haven't happened in other countries.

If someone is denied their legal rights, what could they do to obtain them?

- If a person is denied legal rights based on the UN Universal Declaration of Human Rights, they can probably contact the UN Commissioner for Human Rights to try to get them to put pressure on their national government – or try themselves to get their parliament to incorporate key human rights into the country's legal framework. They could also set up a blog on the Internet to raise awareness.
- However, in repressive countries, the media are often not free and an individual campaigning for such changes, if identified, might be persecuted or killed.
- In Europe most countries have signed up to the European Declaration of Human Rights, sponsored by the Council of Europe (nothing to do with the European Union), so citizens from those countries can go to the European Court of Human Rights in Strasbourg if they cannot get a particular right upheld in their own country's courts.
- Many fewer cases from the UK now have to go to the Strasbourg court since the main provisions of the European Declaration of Human Rights were incorporated into UK law in the Human Rights Act 1998.

CITIZENSHIP STUDIES

Why might moral obligations seem more important than legal responsibility?

- None of us wants to let down our friends or relatives or others we care about – just as we hope they won't let us down.
- Often a concern for others will stem from our religious and ethical values. Many UK people give generously to organisations such as Christian Aid, Oxfam or the Red Cross whenever they issue an appeal to help people caught up in a humanitarian crisis.
- We all have a sense of 'right' and 'wrong'; if we see one person attacking another or stealing their property, there is no law to say we have to try to stop such criminal activity, but many of us would want to try and do so. That is why, when particularly dangerous criminals are about, the police often advise citizens that they should definitely not 'have a go' at the criminal if they see her or him.

Freedom to... and freedom from...

Lesson objectives	Specification link: Unit 1, Theme 1

By the end of this spread the student should:

- be able to recognise the difference between freedom to (do whatever we want) and freedom from (hunger, ignorance, sickness, etc.)

- understand the significance of freedoms of speech, movement, opinion, privacy, association and the vote, how they were obtained and why they are important

- understand why we should not take for granted democracy, justice, diversity, toleration, respect and freedom

Focus

Make sure your students clearly understand (1) the difference between the five giant evils and policy areas to combat each 'evil' (e.g. housing policy to eliminate squalor), (2) the youngest ages at which the law allows individuals to undertake the activities listed and (3) why these two angles are important in the debate over lowering the voting age to 16.

Key terms

- civil partnership
- civil rights
- candidate
- Commission for Equality and Human Rights
- Commonwealth of Nations
- Criminal responsibility
- Democracy

- discrimination
- justice
- poverty
- respect
- tolerance/toleration
- unemployment
- Welfare state

Linked activity sheets

- Big Brother is watching you!
- Who do I trust?
- Design a multicultural town

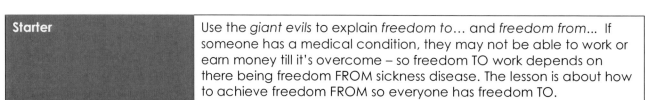

Starter	Use the *giant evils* to explain *freedom to...* and *freedom from...* If someone has a medical condition, they may not be able to work or earn money till it's overcome – so freedom TO work depends on there being freedom FROM sickness disease. The lesson is about how to achieve freedom FROM so everyone has freedom TO.
Development	As a class, discuss with students why freedom TO and freedom FROM are often difficult to achieve. Sometimes we can't afford to do everything so choices have to be made.
	Discuss where these freedoms have come from. Are there other freedoms students think we should have?
	Which of the freedoms listed do students consider most important and why? Remind them about empathy *(how would you feel if...?)*
	Ask students to look at the list of minimum ages and why these might be in place. Are they right – or should some be raised or lowered?

CITIZENSHIP STUDIES

	(Emphasise the importance of knowing these facts for the exam.) Link voting age to this discussion – allow a debate if there is time.
Plenary	Ensure students understand the points in the *Checklist* and the key terms they have encountered.
	For homework, you may wish students to research the *Further issues* questions, or, in preparation for the next lesson, find reasons why people move to Britain from other countries.

Answers to questions in the Student Book

What's the issue?

Why is voting important?
- Voting is how individuals can choose between political parties which offer different policies.
- One party might favour building more houses while another may say your town or village is big enough as it is. One party may favour a congestion charge and improving public transport while another might say people should be free to use their cars and we need more and better roads.
- If we don't take part in elections, have we lost our right to complain if we don't like the way things turn out later on?

Have all 18-year-olds always been able to vote? Should the age when they can work and marry be raised to 18? If 16 year-olds are mature enough to work and marry are they responsible enough to be able to vote?
- Until 1969, the minimum voting age was 21.
- 18, 19 and 20 year olds have been allowed to stand as candidates for elections only since 2007.
- 16-year-olds can work, marry and join the army because they are considered mature enough to do so.
- How could it be justified to say they cannot earn money or get married till they are 18?
- With the school leaving age rising to 18 in coming years, would it matter if 16 year old voters were all schoolchildren? Or would it mean that if consumers of education voted, better decisions would be made?

Margin questions

Why do people leave their home countries to travel and settle in the UK?
- There are 'push' and 'pull factors. Some people want to come to the UK (or elsewhere) to flee oppression in their own country – technically they are asylum seekers – they may want to leave because of a tribal conflict or a tyrant dictator such as Saddam Hussein in Iraq or Robert Mugabe in Zimbabwe or they may fear ethnic or religious persecution (Bosnia, Croatia, Serbia).
- Others want to come to improve their standard of living. Such people are considered to be economic migrants – they often work hard and add to the UK economy, while also sending money back to their home country to support the family they have left behind. UK citizens can work or live in any EU country and people from other EU countries can come to live in the UK. Many UK pensioners choose to go and live in France, Spain or Portugal once they have retired.

Review and research

Can any restrictions on freedom of speech be justified?

YES	NO
- Many religious people believe that the law should protect their religion from blasphemous attacks. Sikhs have protested against plays which attacked their religion and Muslims protested strongly against Salman Rushdi's book The Satanic Verses. - One person's freedom of speech can be at the expense of another person's privacy. Privacy	- In a democracy, people have the right to know about what government and public authorities are doing - that is why the Freedom of Information Act 2000 was passed. - In some oppressive countries people can be punished or even killed for criticising their leaders (e.g. Khmer Rouge in Cambodia); in a democracy such as the UK, people have the

law has increased in importance in recent years so the media and others are now much more restricted than previously in what they can report.
- The law of defamation protects people from individuals who may damage their reputation by saying unfair and untruthful things about them; libel is the term used if the statements are written, slander if they are spoken.

right to freedom of speech and expression, guaranteed by the Human Rights Act 1998.
- The fact that councils and government can be criticised by citizens in the media and blogs on the internet means that free speech guarantees accountability by rulers and ensures there is a vibrant debate over what is right or wrong for society. (Just think about MPs expenses!)

Why should we show tolerance to other people and their values or beliefs?

- If we want to follow a particular lifestyle, support a particular religion and pursue our interests – sport, music, keeping animals or whatever – and not be subject to the judgement of others, then we need to adopt a 'live and let live' approach.
- But we need to be careful not to cause annoyance to others through our activities – we have rights to live our own lives as we wish but we also have responsibilities as citizens to others to respect their values, beliefs and lifestyle choices.
- To avoid problems with the law, we need – for example - to avoid causing annoyance to neighbours through environmental pollution or to not stir up racial or religious hatred if we dislike the religion or ethnicity of others.

How can individuals use democracy and justice to support themselves and their community?

- Democracy involves individuals in participating – as voters, perhaps as supporters of a political party or working with a pressure group. Sometimes people who feel particularly strongly about a certain cause decide to campaign for the changes they favour – sometimes they even stand as candidates to become a councillor or MP or MEP.
- Communities are social networks with a shared interest – often but not always in a particular geographical area. Sometimes an ethnic group will be referred to as a Chinese community or a Polish community in a particular area where people can help and support each other as they become familiar with living in the UK, learning the language, gaining work, sharing child-minding, understanding rights and responsibilities.
- Justice helps to ensure people enjoy the rights they are given through criminal and civil law while also meeting the obligations the laws impose upon them. In a local community local people may be asked to serve as magistrates in courts that deal with 98% of criminal offences in England and Wales. In more serious cases local people are often asked to serve on a jury, deciding the innocence or guilt of an accused person.

CITIZENSHIP STUDIES

Diverse UK

Lesson objectives	Specification link: Unit 1, Theme 1
By the end of this spread the student should be able to recognise: • the relationship between identities and diversity • how and why people have chosen to migrate to and from the UK ('push' and 'pull' factors)	

Focus

Make sure your students clearly understand the differences between economic migrants and asylum seekers and how everyone undertakes many different roles and how a person may have multiple identities – who would a child of a West Indian father and Australian mother brought up in England cheer for when international cricket is on the television?

Key terms

- asylum-seekers
- community/communities
- community integration
- culture
- diversity
- East End
- economic migrant

- ethnicity/ethnicities
- identity
- identities - multiple
- migration – push/pull
- multicultural
- racism
- roles

Linked activity sheets

- What is British?
- Design a multicultural town
- Big Brother is watching you!

Starter	Start off by talking about someone everyone in the class will know – maybe a 'soap' character or another teacher or a well-known former pupil – and highlight some of the person's identities – maybe young/old, male/female, subject teacher/head of year, son/daughter/mother/father... the aim is to get across that we all have many different roles/identities.
Development	Go around the class and brainstorm on the board all the many identities people have and bring out how identities may lead to different loyalties – e.g. to where we live, to particular sports teams or groups, to having different interests, etc.
	Use different interests to build up the idea of communities as being either neighbourhoods or people who are not in close proximity but who have things in common – e.g. ethnicity (Chinese community, Bangladeshi community), team loyalties (e.g. Aston Villa supporters) or shared hobbies (e.g. stamp-collectors, war-gamers, marathon runners) or those with shared experiences (e.g. ex-army personnel). Use these activities to emphasise how different identities may be. How important in all this is wealth and poverty?

CITIZENSHIP STU

	Move on to think about why people move around – either in UK or between different countries. Emphasise the idea of 'push' and 'pull' factors.
	Ask students whether they think the East End was a good example to use – can they think of other multicultural areas that would provide good examples? How diverse is the area where they live or where the school/college is situated?
Plenary	Get the students thinking about the *Checklist* at the end of the spread. At some stage they will need to focus on/research the *Further issues* – could be homework. Round off by getting them thinking about how the *Key terms* help them understand the main points in the spread.

Answers to questions in the Student Book

What's the issue?

Why does the East End have many ethnic restaurants (e.g. Chinese, Turkish, Asian and Vietnamese) and Polish delicatessens?

- Over the years many different groups of refugees have settled in the East End of London, often having arrived at the docks. Typically Hugenots, Jews and more recently Pakistani and Bangladeshi communities have settled and worked in the East End prior to moving on once they could afford better housing.
- The number of different ethnic restaurants reflects the population of the area – those who come from other countries want to stick to many of their traditional foods, so they want to find shops which sell familiar ingredients. This makes it easy to establish restaurants and delicatessens.
- Of all parts of England, the East End may well be the most genuinely multicultural, where there is a celebration of different cultures and a support for them. A particular ethnic community is less likely to be isolated and more likely to be engaged and involved in East End life and the shared customs and tolerance of different faiths which are characteristic there.

Why do you think some parts of the East End are well-off and others are poor?

- As London docklands around the Isle of Dogs and the old West India docks declined with the coming of containerisation and air freight, large parts of the area became almost derelict. Transport links were poor and the cycle of decline was destined to continue.
- This would have continued had a massive programme of expensive riverside housing developments and prestige office building not been promoted by the Conservative Thatcher and Major governments in the 1980s and 1990s, producing iconic buildings such as Canary Wharf.
- Revitalisation of the East End depended on new transport links such as Docklands Light Railway and the Underground Jubilee line extension. Later the area will benefit from infrastructure projects such as Crossrail and all the development associated with the 2012 Olympic Games.
- In the meantime amid such affluence, many of the traditional communities continue to exist in the area causing enormous variations of income, wealth, property ownership patterns and prices, which coexist alongside each other.
- Much of the new East End is located in the London Boroughs of Tower Hamlets and Newham (formerly East Ham and West Ham) where 50% or more of the community may be non-white and from an ethnic minority. A similar proportion of local residents of all colours and faiths depend on rented social housing, reflecting their relatively low levels of income.

Is the East End typical of the rest of the UK?

YES
- Many parts of the UK have richer and poorer areas, though perhaps not coexisting as closely as they do in the East End.
- Many parts of the UK have areas where, like the East End, a high proportion of residents are from ethnic minorities - over 60% in some parts of Birmingham and nearly as high in Leicester but less so in Manchester.

NO
- Differences between rich and poor are probably starker than in most other places of Britain.
- Typically better-off people aspire to live in the leafy suburbs or the countryside, leaving the inner city and the estates to poorer people. In the East End, prestige developments have meant that many richer people want to live on the riverside while poorer people are often crowded into estates of

CITIZENSHIP STUDIES

- Many poorer people living in the East End stay there because all the social, employment and housing changes have provided them with opportunities for work, as much as elsewhere. They are part of London where public transport – although often overcrowded – remains a decided strength and asset to the community.

- former local authority housing.
- More so than other communities elsewhere, which are often more stable in composition, the East End is often where people stay when they first arrive to the UK before they move out into other parts.
- The East End is also different because it is more genuinely multicultural than other urban centres, where minorities may remain relatively isolated rather than sharing each other's customs, faiths and values.

Margin questions

The many ethnic groups in the East End mean it is a multicultural area in which diversity is celebrated. Identify some different forms of cultural diversity in the area where you live.
This will depend on the area, but foods, religion, art, performance, sport, leisure and community activities will all play a part; in some areas, distinctive forms of work may affect the self-image of the community, thus becoming part of its culture, e.g. making jewellery in Birmingham, cider in Somerset, shoes in Northampton, carpets in Kidderminster or pottery in Newlyn.

Who do you think you are? What are the different roles and identities you have?
- Every individual has multiple identities – a man may play the role of son, grandson, father, (perhaps also step-father), uncle, husband, partner, employee, trade union member, member of a professional association (e.g. lawyer, doctor, accountant, lecturer or teacher), church member, coach for the youth football team, member of a former pupils' association of his old school.
- The man may identify more closely with some of these roles than others (father more than uncle, employee more than member of a former pupils' association of his old school), and his self-image or identity may reflect things he wants or aims to do eventually – take part in the Olympic games, own a particular car, win X-Factor, etc.
- Identity will also reflect his roots, including nationality, place of birth, where he lives now and who he cheers for in football or cricket matches.
- How similar would a woman's roles be to those of the man? Would they have the same roles or different ones?

Review and research

Why do racial tensions break out in some areas but not others?
- Probably every incident has causes or circumstances that are special to it.
- One factor which was much discussed following the riots in Burnley and Oldham in 2001 was the isolation and disengagement of some communities, especially where ethnic minority children went to the neighbourhood comprehensive school and most local white children went to a local faith school run by the Church of England or the Roman Catholic Church. Teenagers who otherwise might have had much in common did not know each other and may have seen each other as 'enemies'.
- Often racial tensions break out because they are provoked by extremists, especially in areas where the white working class comes to feel neglected and are encouraged to believe they are in danger of becoming second class citizens in their own country.

Which cultural forms best define the East End today?
- Here the communities of the East End are defined, probably, by exactly the same things as other areas:
  o languages and their literature, poetry, dramas, films and music
  o jobs they do and aspirations for the future
  o friendships, shared values and concern for each other
  o foods and 'special occasions'
  o religions and traditions
  o social, sporting and leisure activities.

CITIZENSHIP STUDIES

Is Britain right to restrict the numbers of economic migrants coming to the country?

YES

- The UK government has accepted since the 1940s the need to provide full employment (spending millions on Job Centres, New Deal and related investment, training and retraining schemes) and that is reason enough not to admit economic migrants to compete for a limited number of jobs.
- The government now identifies the jobs where there are persistent shortages and insufficient skilled workers in the UK and prevents people coming to work in the UK from outside the EU unless they can offer these skills.
- Sometimes people with valuable skills (such as nurses, teachers, doctors) from less economically developed countries want to come and work in the UK. Although we often cannot fill some of these jobs, many overseas communities (e.g. in Africa) would be better off if their own people went back to support them with the professional services they have been trained to provide, rather than seeking to work in the UK.

NO

- Limits on economic migrants coming into the UK apply only to potential migrants who live outside the EU. The EU allows unrestricted movement to live and work in any member country to EU citizens. Like UK citizens going to work abroad, many workers from Poland come to work here for a few years and then return home. If there is intense competition for jobs in the UK they do not stay.
- Before the 2008-2009 credit crunch the UK needed economic migrants to come to the country because there are now more pensioners than children aged up to 16. As people retire, there are not sufficient UK citizens to fill the resulting vacancies.
- It is sometimes argued that, even if we need suitably skilled workers from overseas, we cannot afford to provide the health, housing, education and related services they need; this argument is confused because such workers earn and save and in the long run contribute more to the UK than they take from it.
- Often workers from overseas are willing to do work such as cutting celery or picking fruit, which UK workers will not do even if they are unemployed.

Should the numbers of asylum seekers be limited?

The case for restricting numbers of asylum seekers coming to the UK is much weaker than that for economic migrants. Asylum seekers are fleeing from persecution and oppression. At present, asylum seekers are not allowed to work for money and pay taxes. In April 2007 the Refugee Council commissioned a poll as part of their Strangers into Citizens programme, which showed that two thirds of people think asylum seekers and refused asylum seekers should be allowed to work and pay taxes. The programme campaigns for people who have been in the country for more than four years – both asylum seekers and illegal immigrants – to be given a permit to work legally and pay taxes.

CITIZENSHIP STUDIES

A pick-and-mix society

Lesson objectives	Specification link: Unit 1, Theme 1
By the end of this spread the student should be able to: • understand different kinds of communities living in the UK	

Focus

Make sure your students clearly understand the idea of life expectancy, its main causes and why it may differ greatly between communities that are geographically quite close to each other – they often find this a difficult concept.

Key terms

- citizen
- Citizenship test
- Citizenship ceremony
- constituency
- household
- life expectancy
- professional

Linked activity sheets

- What is British?
- Design a multicultural town

Starter	Start by asking about different places in the area; possibly compare two housing areas or a village and town. Who lives where and why? Answers are likely to include: choice; income; nearness to family, friends or work; what they can afford.
Development	There is a lot of movement in some areas, much less in others. Why do people move house? Answers might include going up (or down) in the world; because of work; some people only ever intend to live in an area for a short time (e.g. students at university). Why might migrants from other countries come/not come to live in your area?
	Extended families all used to live in close proximity – why doesn't this happen any more? Answers might include: more people live a single lifestyle, marrying later if at all; more focus on careers by women; more cohabitation; whereas many people used to go to work in traditional industries in 'their' area, many 'traditional' industries have now declined and more people commute distances to work; people are much less likely to expect to have a 'job for life'.
	What makes life expectancy lower in some areas than others (it can differ by over 10 years in different parts of a city such as Sheffield or Glasgow)? It depends on lifestyle, income/wealth, diet, poverty, job, quality of housing, access to healthcare, and bad habits (e.g. drugs, smoking, excessive alcohol, carrying knives).
	What can someone do to improve their life expectancy? Where we choose to live depends on things we cannot always control. What community organisations help us feel welcome to the area? By deciding whether or not to get involved, e.g. through churches, schools, sports and social groups, people can make a big difference.

CITIZENSHIP STU...

	If people live isolated lives they will probably be lonely and unhappy; if they develop shared interests with others they are more likely to make friends, be accepted and feel much happier.
Plenary	Fit the points above to the *Checklist*. How has the class helped to answer the *Further issues*? Get students thinking about where they would like to live if they could make a free choice, and why.

Answers to questions in the Student Book

What's the issue?

Why so different?
- Generally speaking, the lower the proportion of professional and managerial workers, the lower the average weekly disposable household income and the lower the average property values. This is clearly an economic relationship.
- There is a suggestion that the higher the proportion of non-white citizens in an area, the greater the proportion of social renters occupying mainly council or former council houses. In Leominster and Ludlow there are less than 1% non-white residents, typical of the very rural areas they are.

Which do you think are the rural constituencies?
- The two areas where the non-white population is lowest are most likely the rural constituencies.
- They are Ludlow and Leominster in the very rural counties of Shropshire and Herefordshire respectively.

Which party do you think was elected in each constituency in 2005? Why do you think this was?
- Hodge Hill, Ladywood and Sparkbrook elected Labour MPs; average weekly disposable household income is lowest in these areas (people with lower incomes voting Labour) as are the proportions of professional or managerial workers who typically support the Conservatives or Liberal Democrats. The areas have much the highest figures for social renters, with council estates and former council estates often supporting Labour.
- Leominster, Ludlow and Sutton Coldfield elected Conservative MPs; average weekly disposable incomes here are much higher, as is the proportion of professional and managerial workers.
- Solihull was the one seat where a Liberal Democrat MP was elected; in the past it has elected Conservative MPs as the social indicators would suggest, but not on this occasion – Liberal Democrats tend to draw support more widely from all social groups, so it isn't easy to predict their support from such variables.

What differences do work, income and housing make?
- It is clear that higher income levels are seen as the proportion of professional and managerial workers in an area rises and the higher these two levels, the higher the price of houses will typically be.
- Also, the more social renters in an area, the lower the average weekly disposable income tends to be.
- Consistent with this, we can also see that the lower the proportion of professional and managerial workers (and therefore the more people with working class jobs), the lower house prices are.

Margin questions

About two-thirds of people participate in democratic voting in UK elections. Why do you think they do that? Why do you think some people don't take part?
- Participation needs to be high to keep democracy healthy – all citizens need to take part.
- In the 1950s about 80% voted, so the drop to about 60% in the 2001 and 2005 general elections is disappointing.
- If we leave voting to others, we should not be disappointed if we don't like the result!
- The proportions voting in European and local elections are often less than half the general election proportion. In 2009 many voters deliberately abstained because they were dissatisified.
- Some people may not take part because they feel they do not understand political issues well enough. To help people gain a better understanding is one of the reasons all students now study Citizenship!

CITIZENSHIP STUDIES

- Sometimes people say they do not take part because their vote won't make any difference, yet in 2005 three Labour MPs won with a majority of less than 100 votes out of 50,000 – in Crawley, Harlow and Sittingbourne & Sheppey.
- Often, turnouts are highest where local people feel one party may win the seat from another.

Why did the government decide in 2002 that new arrivals wanting to become British citizens must take a test?

- To become a citizen is not just to live in the UK but to become part of UK society and play an active role in the community, engaging with friends and colleagues at work, at church, in leisure activities or when doing simple things such as picking up children from school.
- After the race riots of 2001 it was felt that, if everyone spoke English, individual members of ethnic minority communities would be less isolated (isolation being seen as a prime source of the discontentment).
- Where people needed to learn English, the process of attending classes to do so meant the individuals would become engaged in UK life with fellow citizens. This could only be good in helping them feel part of society, especially after they had attended their Citizenship ceremony.

Why do you think over 200,000 British citizens went to live in other countries?

- Some will have gone to work in other EU countries.
- Many go to live a different lifestyle with their families in New Zealand, Australia or the USA.
- Many pensioners go to live in warm climates such as Portugal, Spain and France.
- Some now live in France and use Eurostar train services to commute back to the UK to work.

Review and research

How is community integration and a sense of belonging best achieved?

- In the UK, community spirit is often strongest in villages and small towns where people know each other, went to school together, share interests and values and look out for each other if anyone finds themselves in difficulty.
- When such communities have shared goals and campaign hard to achieve them – with everyone pulling together – they can often persuade authorities not to e.g. close the post office or bus service.
- In more urban places there are sometimes residents' committees that try to foster a sense of community, especially if they have a community centre where people can meet, have a drink and engage in leisure activities; if there is not a community centre, local schools or churches often try to fill the gap.
- In urban areas, the sense of community is often much weaker because people move in and move out more regularly.
- Because of this greater social mobility, people are often heard to say they have seen their next-door neighbours but have no idea who lives one house further down the road from them.
- Much social interaction now goes on through blogging and websites such as Facebook.
- The election campaign run by Barack Obama in the USA in 2008 shows that the internet can be a powerful tool in getting people to volunteer and work together to achieve shared goals for themselves and their community.

Why is life expectancy longer in some communities than others?

- Life expectancy reflects material wealth, a good work-life balance, health care, exposure to or avoidance of pollution and also income and lifestyle.
- In some poor African countries, many people are lucky to reach 40 years, barely half the life expectancy for babies born in the UK in 2009. The world average is about halfway between the two.
- In the UK some parts of Glasgow have a life expectancy level near the world average due to factors such as unemployment, poverty, obesity, pollution, poor education, drug abuse, smoking and unhealthy diet.
- In other more affluent parts of the UK, average life expectancy is at least 20 years longer as people are employed or retired, financially secure, health-conscious, well educated and generally have a healthy diet.

Apart from voting, how can people demonstrate support for democracy?

- The most important thing is for people to pay attention.
- They should read their local newspaper and/or look at their Council's website to see what's going on.
- Watching BBC or ITV news broadcasts or even looking at BBC Parliament is a good way of checking what government is doing, in particular whether MPs are debating something of direct relevance.

CITIZENSHIP STUDIES

- If a person feels strongly about an issue they should say so – not just to their friends but perhaps writing a letter to the local paper, writing a blog, phoning a talk-in programme; if they disagree with an MP or councillor, they should write to them and tell them exactly why they disagree.
- A democracy cannot thrive if its people are passive or disengaged rather than aware and involved.
- That's why it is a good idea for people to join organisations – a political party or a pressure group, to give voice to the things that matter to them.
- Joining an organisation is just the first step – democracy works best when lots of people go out campaigning, engaging in social activities and fundraising, acting as a spokesperson or even becoming a candidate for office as a councillor, MP or MEP.

Consumption and employment: Shopping around

Lesson objectives	Specification link: Unit 1, Theme 1
By the end of this spread the student should be able to: • understand the rights and responsibilities of consumers and traders	

Focus

Make sure your students clearly understand the differences (which are often found difficult) between credit, debit and store cards, including the advantages or disadvantages of each. All three are convenient but credit cards can be expensive if the balance is not regularly paid off and store cards can be **very** expensive.

Key terms

- Citizens' Advice Bureau
- consumer
- contract
- credit card
- debit card
- goods

- hire purchase
- interest rate
- personal loan
- services
- store card
- Trading Standards

Starter	Introduce students to the idea of buying and selling and contracts. Ask what contracts they have been involved in today, e.g. with a bus or train company, with a shop if they bought sweets or drink, with the canteen if they bought food, or with a mobile phone company if they phoned home or sent someone a text.
Development	Explain that contracts don't need to be written down and ask why it is a good idea to read them if they are. Use the table to highlight rights, and discuss how to complain. When might you win? What should you do if the law is on your side but the shop won't agree? Get the class thinking about the moral and legal rights involved (see question in Examzone on SB p. 44). What is the best way to pay for goods ☐ cash, pre-pay card, credit card, debit card, store card, personal loan or hire purchase? What happens if you don't pay a credit card bill on time? Discuss when a 'sale' becomes a swindle, e.g. when it is not a 'true' sale at all. Have any of the students worked in a shop? What experiences do they have of dealing with faulty/returned goods, attempted shoplifting or consumer complaints?
Plenary	Fit the points above to the *Checklist*. How has the lesson helped to answer the *Further issues*? Encourage students to think about the best way to get value for money – not spending too much or ending up with inferior goods.

Answers to questions in the Student Book

What's the issue?

Why might it be safer to pay for a big purchase with a credit card?
- The Consumer Credit Acts say that you will probably get your money back from the card issuer if something goes wrong, e.g. if the holiday hotel doesn't live up to the promises in the brochure or if the new computer keeps crashing and won't work.
- The advantage of this arrangement is that if the trader has gone bust and cannot be found or has no money, you will still be compensated by the card company.

What stops a shopkeeper claiming there is a sale on when no prices have really been reduced?
- The Consumer Protection Act 1987 says that when an item is claimed to be in a 'sale', it should have been offered for sale at the higher price in the same shop for at least 28 days in the previous six months.
- By breaking this law a shopkeeper would be exposing themselves to possible penalties.

What rights do you have if you buy a tracksuit and the stitching comes undone the first time you wear it?
- The Sale of Goods Acts make it clear that goods must be of satisfactory quality – and a tracksuit that comes unstitched would be of unsatisfactory quality.
- The shop should give you alternative goods or your money back; otherwise they could find themselves in trouble with Trading Standards.

If a shopkeeper sells you an electric fire saying it was very safe, what is the position when it gives you an electric shock?
- The Supply of Goods and Services Acts makes safety a key requirement of any sale, so the shopkeeper will want to replace the faulty electric fire or give you your money back – always assuming the fault has been evident from the time you purchased the fire.
- If the fire worked perfectly for four years and then gave you an electric shock, this wouldn't apply because no-one expects a product to work perfectly for ever.
- That is why traders often offer extended warranties, though in many cases, after a few years, it is cheaper to buy a new product than spend a lot of money on warranties you may never need.

Margin questions

Consumers who buy goods or services for their own use have many rights. Do sellers have as many rights?
- Sellers have to be sure the goods and services they sell are of appropriate quality and fit for purpose. If they want to avoid receiving complaints and returned goods, they need to be careful deciding which products to stock and which manufacturers to trade with.
- Sellers don't have to accept returned goods if consumers simply change their mind or if someone gives them an identical present.
- Sellers don't have to give refunds or allow consumers to change goods if they have been used for several months and perhaps become damaged through no fault of the manufacturer or supplier.

Work out how much you would have to pay for £100-worth of sports kit if you used a store card charging 22% interest per year and paid £5 per month.
- Exactly how much would have to be paid would depend on the precise terms of the deal, e.g. whether the interest is calculated on the original sum (£100) or on the reducing sum.
- Over a two year period, 22% of £100 could cost £44 and at £5 per month it could take 29 months to pay off the £144.

Which payment methods for purchases are the cheapest and which, most expensive?
- You don't have to pay any interest if you use cash.
- If you pay with a debit card the money is taken straight out of your bank account, so as long as you have enough money in the account, you will pay nothing for the transaction.
- Many credit cards charge you nothing for the first month or so – so if you clear the balance on a credit card before it becomes due, you will not usually be charged interest.

- If you do not clear the whole of your outstanding balance on a credit card, interest payments can mount up.
- As a general rule, interest rates are highest on store cards and some hire purchase deals.

Review and research

How can consumers gain a better understanding of their rights?
- In the light of this Chapter, by studying Citizenship!
- By getting leaflets on consumers' rights from organisations such as the Citizens' Advice Bureau or the Trading Standards Department of their local Council (or by looking at their website).
- By looking at publications by consumer organisations such as Which? or their website.

Do the disadvantages of credit cards outweigh the advantages?
- Credit cards allow you to buy goods now if you cannot easily afford to pay the full amount straight away.
- That is fine if a person has a fluctuating income with more money coming into their bank account in some months than others – or if they have an occasional month with more bills than usual.
- But the danger comes if over several months an individual is not able to pay off their credit card bills in full.
- Interest rates charged by credit cards can be very high, particularly after any low introductory rate has come to an end.
- Credit cards are useful because they give the consumer protection if a purchase goes wrong.
- But the disadvantages probably outweigh the advantages unless the individual clears the balance completely within six months, and especially if they run more than one credit card account at the same time.

Are consumer rights unfairly loaded in favour of consumers against sellers?
- Consumer rights were put in place because it was recognised that many consumers were being unfairly treated by a minority of unscrupulous traders.
- Nowadays, traders who sell goods that are fit for purpose, fairly priced and correctly labelled have nothing to fear from the legislation.
- Rights and responsibilities on both sides of a shopping transaction are now clear, cutting down reasons for complaint on either side.

Working it out

Lesson objectives	Specification link: Unit 1, Theme 1
By the end of this spread the student should be able to: • understand the rights and responsibilities of employers • understand how employment patterns have changed in the UK	

Focus

Make sure your students clearly understand the rights that employees enjoy at work. These can be difficult to grasp fully.

Key terms

- contract of employment
- Disability Discrimination Act 1995
- disciplinary code
- verbal warning
- written warning
- gross misconduct
- dismissal
- discrimination
- Employment Rights Act 1996

- Equal Pay Act 1970
- Health & Safety at Work Acts
- National Minimum Wage Act 1998
- Race Relations Act 1976
- redundancy
- Sex Discrimination Act 1975
- Strike
- trade union

Linked activity sheets

- Individuals and change

Starter	How many of the students have a part-time job? What are 14-16 year-olds permitted to do? What part-time work can they do when they are older? What will they be allowed to do when they are older? Do they have to wear a uniform? Do they have a contract of employment – what does it say?
Development	Focus on the seven laws. Use a discussion about which laws students think are more important, to build up familiarity with all of them. Set up a debate about whether students would join a union if they had a full-time job. Explore pros and cons of union membership. Discuss when a verbal, written or final warning might be justified. What is gross misconduct – how bad does behaviour at work have to be to get sacked? Make sure everyone understands the difference between dismissal and redundancy.
Plenary	Match the points above to the *Checklist*. How has the lesson helped to answer the *Further issues*? Ask students to think about what kind of job they would like to do if they could make a free choice – and why they made that choice.

Answers to questions in the Student Book

What's the issue?

How do the patterns of trade union membership for men and women differ?

- The graph shows that men used to have a higher rate of trade union membership than women but that since 2000 the proportion of men and women who belong to trade unions has been between 25% and 30% for both men and women, with women being slightly ahead in 2006.
- Full-time employees were more likely to be union members than part-time employees, at 31.0 and 21.2 per cent respectively – and more women work part-time than men.
- Trade union membership is typically highest in areas with industries such as coal mining and manufacturing. The majority of members there are male, though a large proportion of the membership of the public sector workers union, Unison (covering local government and the NHS), is female.
- Females joining trade unions often do so to get equal pay for equal work or to ensure they have an organisation to help them receive their employment rights.
- More than a third of employees aged 35 and over were union members, compared with a quarter of those aged between 25 and 34.

Why are some workers more or less likely to join a union than others?

- Between 70% and 75% of workers do not belong to a trade union in the UK.
- Other workers may come from families which have always believed in joining a union and wish to continue to do so.
- In some workplaces, fellow workers may put pressure on everyone to join the union.
- Trade union membership has fallen as workers are less likely to expect to work for the same firm for the whole of their working life.
- Many younger workers enjoy the flexibility of working on short-term contracts for which pay and working conditions are known in advance and agreed, leaving little for a trade union to negotiate about – and giving the workers no reason to join a union.
- The fact that there is much higher trade union membership in the North East of England (where employment has largely been based on heavy industries) than in the South East of England (where employment is largely based on service industries) reminds us that trade union membership is often a matter of local history and tradition.
- Where there is little or no local history of prolonged battles over pay and working conditions, many employees nowadays may see little point in joining a trade union.

What are the arguments for and against going on strike to settle a dispute?

- If negotiations between employers and employees break down, workers are faced with the choice of going on strike or only performing certain duties, or backing down.
- Whether or not workers are willing to back down, depends on how strongly they feel about the issues over which they are fighting.
- Going on strike will probably mean receiving no pay while not at work and this can cause great hardship to workers and their families, especially if a strike is prolonged. If unions have sufficient funds, they sometimes give small financial handouts to strikers.
- Even when workers go on strike, an agreement has to be negotiated eventually between employers' and employees' organisations.
- Employers generally don't want activity to come to a halt and therefore try to avoid strikes if they can.
- The government often tries to get the two sides in a dispute to agree to arbitration via an impartial organisation such as ACAS (the Advisory, Conciliation and Arbitration Service).

Margin questions

On average, workers in the UK work more hours than workers in other EU countries. Is this good or bad?

- The advantage for UK workers is that they can work more hours if they wish to do so.
- This is said to give employers greater flexibility, so they can call on employees to work overtime when things get busy.
- Many people believe workers in the UK work far more hours than is good for their health.

- The workaholic tendency can mean people don't get the 'work-life balance' right, which is bad for both themselves and their families.
- At times when there is a shortage of jobs, it could be argued that if everyone worked less – say for 30 hours a week – this would be better than some having no job while others work for 40 or 50 hours a week.

Is it fair that compensation for redundancy, linked to the number of weeks' pay per year of service, should vary for different age groups?

- The argument in favour of having higher rates of redundancy pay according to age may reflect the reality that older workers are likely to find it harder to get a new job and their long service means they have made a significant commitment to the firm.
- It could be said, though, that older workers already get significantly higher pay than younger workers, so is there a possibility that young workers are in effect being unfairly penalised (a smaller percentage of low pay) compared with the higher percentage of higher pay for older workers?

Review and research

Why are so many fewer workers now members of trade unions?

- During the 1980s, when many workers felt their rights were being threatened by government legislation, a natural thought was to defend one's rights by joining a union.
- As a result of the Labour government elected in 1997, challenges to workers' rights were no longer on the agenda, so union membership became less of a priority.
- Indeed, it may be that now only the most committed supporters of trade unions feel the need to join.

Have employment laws improved the experience of working in the UK?

- The improvements to employment arrangements in the UK over recent years can be seen from the provisions of the main employment legislation.
- Disability Discrimination Act 1995: aims to end discrimination against disabled people, particularly in employment – prior to the Act, such discrimination did occur.
- Employment Rights Act 1996: deals with the rights that most employees can expect when they work, including protection against unfair dismissal, reasonable notice before dismissal, time-off rights for parenting and redundancy pay. Amendments since 1997 have included the right to request flexible hours.
- Equal Pay Act 1970: says women and men doing the same or similar work should get equal pay and benefits. Although there is concern that this law has, even in 2009, not fully achieved equal pay for equal work, the 'gap' is now significantly less than when the Act was passed.
- Health & Safety at Work Acts: are intended to ensure that the workplace is a safe working environment.
- National Minimum Wage Act 1998: established the minimum wage in the UK, which is upgraded each year.
- Race Relations Act 1976: forbids employers from treating a person such as an applicant for appointment or promotion less favourably because of their race, colour, nationality or ethnicity. Such discrimination is very much less likely to occur now than when the Act was first passed.
- Sex Discrimination Act 1975: established guidelines for fair employment practices and gave those treated unfairly because of gender or sexual orientation the support of the Commission for Equality and Human Rights.

Should the number of hours per week an employee works be restricted?

- If the number of hours a person is allowed to work for any one firm is restricted, there is the possibility that some people will get one or more part-time jobs with other employers.
- What is important is that UK workers should recognise that too much work leads to stress – and the best way to avoid such problems is to maintain a healthy 'work-life balance'.

CITIZENSHIP STUDIES

Where did our rights & freedoms come from: The United Nations

Lesson objectives	Specification link: Unit 1, Theme 1
By the end of this spread the student should: • know about the UN Universal Declaration of Human Rights, the work of the UN Council on Human Rights and the importance of the UN Convention on the Rights of the Child.	

Focus

Make sure students understand that in some countries human rights are considered less important than in most Western countries, and that human rights are not built into the legal system, so there is little opportunity to provide redress for aggrieved citizens.

Key terms

• Children's Commissioners

• conscience

• cultural values

• discrimination

• genocide

• Human Rights Commissioner

• social inclusion

• UN Council on Human Rights

• UN Convention on the Rights of the Child

Starter	The *What's the issue?* gives just two articles. Brainstorm with students other human rights they might expect to be included.
Development	Look at the full list of rights in the UN Universal Declaration – but focus on why these may be taken more seriously in some parts of the world than others. Think about how the Human Rights Commissioner can pressurise governments. Think also about the activities and effectiveness of other groups, such as Amnesty International or Human Rights Watch. Highlight the problem of rich powerful countries (such as China) often seeming to deny human rights; how far should other countries challenge what happens in another country? How would people in the UK feel if other countries tried to tell us what we should or should not do?
Plenary	Carefully work through the questions in the *Checklist*. You need to get across the idea that, although human rights are not always acknowledged everywhere, there has been great progress over the last 60 years – the position now is very different from what it would have been if the UN had not produced and promoted the Universal Declaration in 1948.

Answers to questions in the Student Book

What's the issue?

Which countries have failed to apply these rights and make them part of their legal code?
Asian and African countries are often less keen on human rights than Western countries. Freedom of speech and expression is often denied, to the extent that little or no publicity is given to the opinions of those who oppose current governments (as in China or Russia).

How well do these rights 'work' for UK citizens?
- In the UK new laws have recently been passed to prevent incitement to racial or religious hatred.
- If a religion involves practices that are contrary to UK law (such as female circumcision or trying to suppress Salman Rushdie's *The Satanic Verses*), they will be subject to legal action.
- Even if everyone has the right to work, that does not mean everyone has a job.
- Although the UK has laws to outlaw discrimination and to provide equal pay for equal work, such laws do not always prove to be totally effective, e.g. many men are still paid more than women for identical work.

What other rights do you think people are entitled to? When you have thought about this, see how many of your ideas are listed in the Declaration.
- Students will probably have identified issues such as: freedom from discrimination; the right to life; liberty and security of person; freedom from being held in slavery or servitude; freedom from torture or cruel, inhuman or degrading treatment or punishment; freedom from arbitrary arrest, detention or exile; freedom from arbitrary interference with a person's privacy, family, home or correspondence, and from attacks upon reputation.
- Everyone has the right to the protection of the law against interference or attacks; the right to health and education is also important – with a requirement that education shall be free, at least in the elementary and fundamental stages, with elementary education being compulsory.
- A complete list can be found on the UN website.

Margin questions

We saw in *All about you* and in *Chapter 1* that human rights need to become legal rights and be included in a country's laws, so why have many countries been slow to act?
- Some countries do not give human rights as much priority as others. Even where laws are passed, they are not always wholly effective (e.g. discrimination and equal pay in UK) and may have been directly flouted in the UK or USA, e.g. the torture of suspected terrorists.
- The culture of some other countries may place greater emphasis on authority, hierarchy or adherence to traditional practices, so there is resistance to the relatively new idea of human rights, e.g. the idea of 'equality' between men and women and between people of different ethnicities is controversial in some parts of the world; also, in the UK the idea of amputating the hands of criminals is abhorrent but that may be an important part of the value system in countries which maintain such practices.

Which four criticisms of the UK over the treatment of children were most important? What should be done about them?
All seven criticisms are serious and it is difficult to say one is more important than another – the debate should enable students to tease out the significance of these points.

Review and research

Can countries rightly regard it as no-one else's business whether their citizens have human rights?
- All countries are sovereign states and so can decide what happens in their own country.
- However, recent economic problems have emphasised how much countries depend on each other.
- This gives countries with concerns the opportunity to put pressure on other regimes which are thought to be misbehaving (e.g. Zimbabwe, Myanmar).
- Sometimes the rest of the world can impose economic sanctions on countries with a poor human rights record. However, there have been many examples of sanctions being overcome by informal deals behind the scenes, suggesting such sanctions need to be policed more actively.

CITIZENSHIP STUDIES

Should the UN intervene actively if countries fail to meet recognised standards of human rights?

- If some world citizens are being denied their human rights, the UN must indicate its disapproval and try to put pressure on the government of the country to improve.
- Just as the International Criminal Court is now starting to try cases involving the most serious crime - genocide – hopefully breaches of human rights will also lead to court actions in future years among countries which have signed up to the Universal Declaration (as the European Court of Human Rights ensures for its 41 member countries in Europe).

Is 'human rights' a Western idea which contradicts the traditional culture and values of other countries?

- This was undoubtedly much truer in 1948 than it is now.
- As communications improve and Sky or BBC or CNN television news appears on screens in every continent, the spread of Western ideas has grown. Although such values may have outraged some, the overall effect has been for more countries to adopt human rights policies, often following pressure by the UN Human Rights Commissioner.

Europe

Lesson objectives	Specification link: Unit 1, Theme 1
By the end of this spread the student should understand: • the European Convention on Human Rights • the European Court of Human Rights • the European Court of Justice	

Focus

While the European Court of Justice is part of the European Union (with 27 member countries), the European Convention of Human Rights and the European Court of Human Rights are part of separate organisation, the Council of Europe (with 41 member countries). Focus particularly on how individuals access rights and on the variable interpretation of a term such as 'degrading'.

Key terms

• capital punishment/death penalty

• community sentence

• corporal punishment/birching

• degrading treatment

• liberty

• McLibel Two/ D Morris and H Steel

• pressure group

• respect

Starter	Should people sentenced to do community work as a punishment be shamed by being made to wear a distinctive uniform (see also page 45 of the textbook)? Is this humiliating or degrading for the criminals or does it give satisfaction to victims and help to reassure everyone else that offenders are being punished?
Development	What can we learn from the case of the McLibel Two? Emphasise the importance of the Richardson case, to show how the European Court of Justice can improve things for large numbers of UK citizens, though not specifically focused on human rights. In 2005, the European Court of Human Rights ruled that men and women serving terms in UK prisons should still be entitled to vote. This is very unpopular with prison officers and the general public and to date in 2009 the UK government has done nothing about it. What are the arguments for and against? Focus on the rights given in the European Convention; ask students to think about what they mean and which are most important.
Plenary	Focus on the points in the *Checklist*. Get the class to think about how they would feel if they were being denied human rights and if there were no ways they could appeal to get justice.

Answers to questions in the Student Book

What's the issue?

Do you agree it is right to ban inhuman or degrading treatment?
In the Middle Ages, people could be hanged, beheaded or burned – all actions we would regard as inhuman and degrading today. Flogging took place in prisons until 1948 and caning continued in some private schools till the 1990s. Such actions are now thought inappropriate because we have a greater appreciation for peoples' rights and freedoms. Students need to explore reasons for and against this.

How would you feel if you could be subjected to such punishments?
It is sometimes suggested that corporal punishment gets a matter dealt with quickly; most students may feel that if they could still be subjected to such punishments they might be careful how they behaved so they wouldn't have to experience them. From a Citizenship point of view, though, people should behave well because it is the right thing to do, not out of fear of a particular punishment.

Should rights be expressed in more definite terms, so they are easier for judges to interpret consistently?
Values change over time. The death penalty was seen as punishment for murder, just like corporal punishment for violence in the past. Whether the terms such as 'degrading' used in official documents are capable of interpretation (or not), the important point is that changes in values are meant the way situations are addressed may change over time.

Margin questions

In the future, could people think it's degrading to send people to prison and lock them in small rooms (sometimes with other prisoners and no privacy) for over 22 hours a day?
Putting a person in a cage or a very small room (like a prison cell) or very close to others is not seen as degrading in 2009 but, as values change, it could come to be seen as degrading in the future. What is 'degrading' can be interpreted by a judge. This means that if a case were made for confinement in prison to be regarded as degrading, the court will have to give a ruling knowing that this surely would become adopted for future cases.

Are there other phrases in the European Convention that could be interpreted in different ways by different judges? What human rights in the Convention may clash?
- When the convention speaks of 'freedom of religion', it does not guarantee a person's right to follow all or any practice of the religion.
- A right to a 'fair trial' is also guaranteed but the meaning of 'fair trial' might vary from one person to another.
- Freedom of movement and the right to work can clash, as do the right of privacy and freedom of expression.

What would be the advantages of taking a case to a UK court rather than the European Court of Human Rights?
To get a case decided in the UK is generally quicker, cheaper and more convenient.

Why do you think two European courts have been established instead of one?
The European Court of Justice deals with disputes in relation to EU law, while the European Court of Human Rights considers cases based on the European Convention of Human Rights. The EU laws and the European Convention of Human Rights have no formal links and it is therefore appropriate that cases are dealt with by different bodies.

Review and research

What does 'degrading' mean in the European Convention?
The term suggests humiliation and not showing respect to an individual. Some people might believe that wrong-doers should be shamed and humiliated; however, if wrong-doers are to be rehabilitated as

members of society, this is more likely to be achieved if, as their offending behaviour is addressed, they are accorded a level of dignity as a human being.

In what ways do both European courts assist UK citizens?

The European Court of Human Rights allows people to claim rights which they feel they have been denied by their own government, assuming their country is one of the signatories to the convention. The rulings of the Court are binding on national governments. Similarly, as Mr Richardson found in the prescription charges case, when he found that men in the UK were being treated differently from women, he was able to go to the European Court of Justice in Luxembourg to get a ruling which said men and women must be treated equally as far as prescription charges are concerned.

Does Europe need both the European Court of Human Rights and the European Court of Justice?

The workload of both courts suggests that there is more than enough for both of them to do, although the demands on the European Court of Human Rights in Strasbourg have been reduced since the 1998 Human Rights Act came into force in the UK. This now deals with many cases that might previously have gone to the Strasbourg Court.

CITIZENSHIP STUDIES

1998 Human Rights Act

Lesson objectives	Specification link: Unit 1, Theme 1
By the end of this spread the student should: • know how UK citizens can claim their rights • know how rights are safeguarded at a local, national or global level	

Focus

Focus on how the Human Rights Act changed the human rights position in the UK, why it is controversial and how the state of human rights in the UK compares with other countries.

Key terms

• crimes against humanity

• custody

• discrimination

• divorce

• declaration of incompatibility

• equal opportunities

• equality

• genocide

• moral panic

Linked activity sheets

• Wants and needs

Starter	Ask students to discuss EM's case as a whole class or in groups. How would they feel or want to act in this situation?
Development	Get a list of the main articles of the Human Rights Act (or use the summary in *All about you*) and explore ways in which the students believe these could help them or their families in different situations.
	Some of the most fruitful provisions for a good discussion could be: • Everyone has the right to life. • No one can be tortured or punished in a degrading way. • No one can be punished for an action which was not a crime when it was committed. • Everyone has the right to privacy and family life. • Everyone has the right to freedom of opinions, beliefs and religion. • Everyone has the right to freedom of speech and expression. • Men and women have the right to marry and have children. • Everyone has the right to own and enjoy their property. • No one is to be denied the right to an education.
	Compare the position of UK citizens with that of people elsewhere in the world. You could use the Human Rights Watch website (http://www.hrw.org/) to find recent cases drawn to the attention of the UN Human Rights Commissioner. Students should research other countries and their human rights records.
	Also, refer to progress in the trials at the International Criminal Court or the Special Tribunals, such as the one dealing with genocide in the former Yugoslavia.

| Plenary | Go over the *Checklist* points. Students could work on the *Further issues* questions as research or homework, or investigate the Commission for Equality and Human Rights and its activities. |

Answers to questions in the Student Book

What's the issue?

Do you think this was the right decision? Is it fair on the father?
- There are many issues and decisions here.
- The father was wrong to try to abduct the boy to Lebanon and was wrong to subject EM to extreme violence.
- Whether Islamic law in Lebanon is right to automatically give custody of a boy to the father once he is 7, reflects different values at work; that is not a policy or a law that operates in the UK.
- EM left Lebanon without permission – but should a person need permission to want to travel abroad?
- EM fears ill treatment and possible death in a Lebanese prison. Surely all prisons should uphold the law – murdering someone can never be right, no matter what offence they have committed.
- How realistic are or were such fears; was she truly in danger?
- EM did not believe she would keep custody of her son after he was 7 if they remained in Lebanon – but perhaps fathers are better than mothers at bringing up boys?
- Was EM right to claim asylum and were the courts which denied her asylum right or wrong in their decisions?
- On 2008, the House of Lords upheld EM's appeal. She had relied on the provision in the European Convention on Human Rights and the Human Rights Act that the right to respect in private and family life is guaranteed.
- As in all instances of marital breakdown, there is inevitably pain on both sides. Would a boy be better placed with his father? Did the father forego his right to his son because of the violence he is said to have directed to his wife?
- Was the Human Rights Act helpful, or not?

Margin questions

Are newspapers and others justified in criticising the Act?
- Newspapers (as Theme 2, Chapter 5 shows in the discussion of 'moral panics') love to scapegoat or demonise particular groups of individuals, sometimes with little or no cause.
- When the European Court of Human Rights ruled that convicted prisoners should not lose their right the vote, the newspapers were quick to criticise.
- In such questions as these there will rarely be an answer to which all agree.
- The best approach is probably to use 'empathy' to get students to think about how they would feel if they were the person whose rights were being protected – that should get them to understand that rushing too quickly to criticise can be a mistake.

What does the Commission for Equality and Human Rights (CEHR) do and how does it help people?
The Commission does the work formerly done by the Commission for Racial Equality, the Disability Rights Commission and the Equal Opportunities Commission. Recent examples of its activities in helping people can be found on its website.

Review and research

Can good reasons ever justify bad actions?
- This question often gets us deep into moral issues.
- Is it all right for the mother of a hungry child to steal to feed her child?
- Is it justifiable to torture a suspected terrorist to get information so that plots are discovered and society is made safe for everyone?
- In reality stealing is always wrong, particularly in a welfare society where there are many ways in which poor people can be guaranteed a sufficient income.
- However, there are people who sometimes don't receive the benefits they are entitled to.

- Equally, torturing people for any reason has to be wrong – the information it yields cannot be used in court, may not be reliable and is likely to recruit more people to the cause of the tortured person.

How is access to more rights likely to affect a person's identity?

If a person is able to access education, healthcare, family life, work and property, they are likely to feel a greater sense of self-confidence and ability to participate in society than if they are denied some or all of these rights.

What service does the Citizens Advice Bureau provide in your area?

Both through local branches and the CAB website (http://www.adviceguide.org.uk/), the CAB is the best impartial and independent source of information about rights and entitlements covering government-sponsored services, local authority services and other services including bankruptcy, employment, discrimination, citizenship applications, pensions and housing.

Why have some countries such as the USA failed to join the International Criminal Court?

Under President George W Bush it was clear the US administration did not want any of its citizens to be subject to extradition proceedings on behalf of the International Criminal Court. Although it is clear that President Barack Obama will review the policy, the outcome of such a review is not known at the time of writing. In the past, the USA has been concerned that attempts might be made by its adversaries to charge some of its soldiers fighting overseas with the types of offences dealt with by the court.

CITIZENSHIP STUDIES

Can our rights be overruled?
If we don't live up to our responsibilities...

Lesson objectives	Specification link: Unit 1, Theme 1
By the end of this spread the student should: • recognise the link between rights and responsibilities • understand how both rights and responsibilities are challenged	

Focus

Make sure students understand how rights and responsibilities go together – if a person doesn't behave responsibly, can they expect to be able to access their rights? Also, ensure they recognise the balance between one person's right versus another person's responsibility, as in the Evans/Johnston case.

Key terms

• eviction

• NHS constitution

• obesity

Linked activity sheets

• Who do I trust?

• Heart transplant

Starter	Encourage students to think about who should pay for NHS healthcare. If boxing is dangerous and a boxer is injured should he or she be required to have insurance to pay NHS bills or should the NHS pick up the bills because the boxer has paid taxes like everyone else?
Development	Does the same apply to motor racing drivers, mountaineers, smokers or people who are obese? If the NHS runs out of money, should services to those who deliberately put themselves in danger be curtailed to make sure treatment can be given to others?
	What's the issue? says that North Staffordshire health trusts now refuse to treat obese patients not because they have behaved irresponsibly as a result of their lifestyle choice to over-eat but because their obesity adds to the risks of operations and may well make treatment less effective. Are these good enough reasons to deny treatment?
	Are there other ways in which rights might be withdrawn if a person behaves irresponsibly?
	Students should also consider how one person's alleged right to play loud music may deny someone else's right to live quietly – how should such considerations be resolved? Is it right to evict people who play noisy music without considering others?
	In groups, students could tease out the rights and responsibilities in the Natallie Evans and Howard Johnston case.

Plenary	Go over the *Checklist* points. You may want the students to work on the *Further issues* questions as research or homework, or they could think about how rights and responsibilities might be balanced in other topic areas, such as education or the environment.

Answers to questions in the Student Book

What's the issue?

Should we deny the *right* to medical treatment to people who don't behave *responsibly* (e.g. putting themselves at risk by excessive drinking, eating too much or smoking)?

- Excessive drinking, over-eating or smoking may be addictions which the NHS should help people to overcome.
- There are often consequences to actions we take – if a person is determined to claim their right to drink, smoke or over-eat, rejecting medical help or advice, the NHS is entitled to deny them treatment until they start to behave responsibly if their behaviour renders treatment more dangerous or less effective.
- Children were upset in 2009 when a series of adverts were shown on television with children watching a parent smoking and saying they feared the parent would die as a result. Smoking parents wanted the adverts withdrawn, yet it could be argued that such adverts were aimed at saving lives and that those who wanted them removed didn't want to face up to the consequences of their own life-threatening behaviour or the trouble their consciences caused them as a result.
- If the NHS is short of funds, should they concentrate resources on those who behave responsibly rather than those who don't? Or should those who add to the chance of making themselves ill be charged extra for treatment?

What attitude should the NHS take to people who deliberately put themselves in danger, such as racing drivers or boxers?

- Insurance companies already have to pay the costs of treatment and ambulance services to the NHS in respect of road traffic accident victims who go on to seek compensation. Would it be appropriate to make the same kinds of charges for those who deliberately put themselves in danger?
- Or should we take the view that life is for living and that the NHS exists to treat us whatever we do, as long as we have made our National Insurance contributions?

Margin questions

- The judges balanced Natallie's right to private and family life with the responsibility which would have been imposed on Howard as the genetic father, a role he did not wish to have now the relationship had broken up. Did they make the right decision in either law or ethics?
- The judges are responsible for interpreting the law in the UK and sometimes their judgements are challenged on moral grounds. Natallie was very upset by Howard's decision not to agree because the embryos offered her the only opportunity to become a biological mother and have a child. The judge decided that as the father, Howard had as much right to decide to have a child as Natallie; thus, this gave him a right to stop the embryos being used. So the judges' decision respected the concern for a baby to have a father and the need for Howard to be willing to undertake the responsibility of parenthood. When he wasn't willing to do that, it would have been ethically difficult for them to allow Natallie to go ahead and have the baby.

Review and research

If you contribute to your own illness, should you expect the NHS to help you get better?

- If a person has an addiction, it is reasonable for the NHS to try to help them overcome it.
- Patients have the right to expect the NHS to help them get better as long as they behave in a responsible way.
- If they do not show responsibility in their actions, their rights to treatment may be curtailed, especially if they ignore the professional advice they are given to overcome their illness.

- However, professional opinion may be wrong, and if so, may not help people to overcome additions for example.

If you play loud music, is it fair on those who are sitting near you on a bus or who live near you?

How would you feel if you were a victim of someone else's loud music? Empathy is an essential factor here and should result in people showing respect and consideration to others. Often those who behave thoughtlessly or selfishly believe they can do whatever they wish, regardless of others – behaving like bullies. Already some councils evict such people from their houses if they are a nuisance to neighbours. Should train and bus companies make them leave the bus or train if they persist in annoying others on their journey?

How much should we consider others? For example, should owners of cars that pollute the environment pay more tax than those who don't?

If we expect our own needs to be considered, we should show consideration to others. The principle of 'polluter pays' is already evident in car tax rates. People need to accept responsibility for the pollution they cause.

CITIZENSHIP STUDIES

A justification for identity-checking, surveillance or detention?

Lesson objectives	Specification link: Unit 1, Theme 1
By the end of this spread the student should: • understand how fears of terrorism may lead to the restriction of rights and freedoms • understand the arguments for and against restricting those rights and freedoms	

Focus

Make sure students understand the ways in which ID cards could help protect UK citizens against identity fraud, illegal working and organised crime. They also need to understand the views of opponents: that government officials have a bad record in losing data; that often government IT projects don't work; that ID cards would not have prevented the London bombings; and that they may actually add to the problems of identity theft.

Key terms

• closed circuit television

• identity

• identity fraud

• multiple identities

• organised crime

• surveillance society

Linked activity sheets

• Big Brother is watching you!

• Reducing the potential for crime in your area

Starter	Using the text, make sure students understand each of the key terms and that some people see ID cards as keeping us safe while others believe any attack on civil liberties makes us weaker.
Development	Start by asking students to think about how fears of danger (identity theft, terrorism, fears of violence) may have caused people to change their behaviour and why the government and police impose restrictions on us: • We all need to try to keep our computers secure from virus attacks and from being bugged. • We need to be secretive about passwords which can access bank details, etc. • CCTV cameras watch us on train stations in shops and town centres. • Limits are placed on travel and the luggage we can take on planes. • People who may be 100% innocent can be imprisoned in the UK for 28 days without charge, much longer than in other countries. • Children are more closely controlled now and are not allowed to go out to play for fear of being attacked, molested or killed. Can students think of other ways in which our freedom of action has been restricted? Then consider whether ID cards would help to overcome fears or threats. In what ways would an ID card do more than a driving

	licence or passport? Could precautions against terrorism cause us to lose the freedoms which make the UK a good place to live?
Plenary	Go over the *Checklist* points. You may want the students to work on the *Further issues* questions as research or homework. Alternatively, they could look at the Information Commissioner's website to check on most recent developments.

Answers to questions in the Student Book

What's the issue?

What is the aim for ID cards?
The idea is that ID cards prove who we are and reveal a deception if we claim to be someone else. However, terrorists often want to be recognised and don't try to hide who they are.

Will ID cards compromise people's privacy but not deter terrorists or criminals?
- If we all had to carry ID cards and show them every time someone asked to see them, this would be taking us towards a dictatorship, with our every move possibly being recorded. Privacy would certainly be compromised.
- It isn't clear whether terrorists or criminals would be deterred and few people doubt that ID cards wouldn't quickly be forged.

Why do we need ID cards? Isn't it enough to produce a driving license or passport to prove who we are?
Few people deny that new technologies which allow identity of criminals to be detected from DNA are a big step forward. But should the data of innocent people be kept on DNA databases? Or should everyone's data be recorded as a matter of course? These steps might make it easier to detect criminals. An ID card with finger prints or a photo that could match the holder against iris-recognition software could help to prove whether an individual is who they claim to be. But is it acceptable to demand photos and finger prints from every citizen? And could wrong-doers outwit such a system?

Margin questions

Young people often complain that they are stopped and searched too often by police. Would official ID cards overcome this problem?
- ID cards would not prevent anyone being stopped, and if they are thought to be carrying illegal drugs or knives, etc., an identity card wouldn't stop them being searched.
- It would help young people prove who they are and so cut down the time confirming identity, but only if people always carry their ID card; otherwise it would cause more problems.
- In future, could it be an offence not to carry your ID card at all times?

How much privacy would a citizen truly have if information from speed and CCTV cameras, records from transactions using store, bank and credit cards and recordings of every telephone call, text and email were all collected together?
Very little, if any. This is why the 'surveillance society' is seen as such a big threat to privacy. It may be that an individual is doing nothing wrong in the eyes of the law, but once an apparatus has been set up to bring all such data together, a tyrannical leader could use it to great ill-effect.

Review and research

How justified are our hopes and fears over the introduction of ID cards?
- A system which can record almost every detail of an individual's activities is a threat to her or his privacy and, in extreme circumstances, could be used to persecute people who resist fitting into a conformist model.
- That is not proposed at present but if such systems did develop, it might be too late to resist them once they were in existence.

- Whether ID cards could keep us safe from terrorism seems doubtful in the light of Madrid and London bombings.

Is the UK in danger of sacrificing too many rights in an attempt to resist terrorism?

- The answer to this question depends on how great one believes the threat of terrorism to be.
- It may be that government restrictions make it more difficult for terrorists to make bombs from particular ingredients or travel on trains or planes, but that doesn't mean they will give up on the attempt to cause trouble.
- That will only happen if they come to see terrorist activity as unnecessary.
- Perhaps governments need to think more about how the causes of terrorism can be challenged.
- In the meantime, can ANY reductions in civil liberties EVER be justified in a free society?

Can intensive surveillance ever be justified or is it an affront to our right of privacy?

Watching someone who is suspected of planning a crime can obviously be justified but watching everyone for no reason except that they might be planning to do something unlawful is much harder to justify and is certainly an intrusion into their personal privacy.

CITIZENSHIP STUDIES

Does religion divide or unite society?

Lesson objectives	Specification link: Unit 1, Theme 1
By the end of this spread the student should:	
• understand how different faiths have different beliefs and traditions	
• understand how far believers are entitled to go to defend or promote their faith	

Focus

Consider whether some people speak of religious differences when really they are engaging in a covert form of racism. Focus also on the religious dimension and the dangers of different groups in society having little contact or dialogue with each other, allowing enmities and misunderstandings to arise, which can cause rioting as in Oldham, Bradford and Burnley in 2001. This partly involved students from faith schools and those from comprehensive schools (including many ethnic minority youngsters) who had little or no contact or empathy with each other.

Key terms

• blasphemy

• culture

• discrimination

• faith schools

• multicultural

• tolerance

Linked activity sheets

• Big Brother is watching you!

Starter	Think about the differences between Northern Ireland before the Good Friday Agreement (different religions emphasising boundaries, differences and discontents) and celebrations such as the Notting Hill or Handsworth Carnivals (differences minimised and different communities coming together for a multi-cultural celebration).
Development	Everyone can practise the religion of their choice but they must not break UK law, e.g. by stirring up racial or religious hatred.
	How realistic is it to see Protestants and Catholics as 'rival tribes' at a Celtic v Rangers match?
	All religions have symbols, some of which may be provocative to people from other religions. In France, Muslim girls cannot wear headscarves in schools. Could the UK have similar rules – perhaps banning people from wearing crosses as a symbol of Christian faith?
	Breaking laws cannot be justified, but perhaps laws should be more sensitive to the cultural traditions of UK residents who have come from other countries with different religious values?
	Or is it reasonable to expect those who live in the UK to live according to UK traditions, cultures and ways or doing things?
	How can people learn to become tolerant of each other's faith and values?

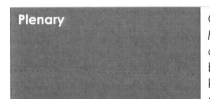

Plenary	Go over the *Checklist* points. You may want students to work on the *Further issues* questions as research or homework, or they could consider whether all faiths and religions need to be celebrated because it is difficult to accept people and their ideas if you do not know them. Harmony depends on respecting and trusting others and, perhaps, sharing in their celebrations.

Answers to questions in the Student Book

What's the issue?

Why are some religions not included in faith groups in some areas?
- There may be historical, doctrinal or personal reasons.
- There may be a desire by Christian faiths to work together but not with others.
- Some church members in a particular community may not want to be involved with people from other faiths.

How similar or different are the beliefs and practices of different religions?
- Some are summarised in *What's the issue*?
- Some are particular to a specific religion, such as dietary rules among Jewish people, the requirement that males be circumcised, or the regularity of prayer among Muslims.
- Often, however, there are considerable variations in attitudes and practices between people in the same religion – some are stricter over rules or observances than others.

Are different religious groups sufficiently tolerant in their responses to people they disagree with?
- Sometimes, but not always.
- Tolerance means we accept others as honestly holding a set of beliefs and respect them for practising their faith even if we do not share their values.
- Dialogue is always beneficial, as long as we can see the benefit of 'agreeing to differ' on doctrine.

Margin questions

How do different ethnic groups acquire UK values and learn about UK laws?
The key is integration into UK society. For those who choose to apply for UK citizenship, preparing for and taking the test on *Life in the UK* will help them become more integrated. Also, it will be difficult for people from ethnic minorities not to acquire awareness of UK laws and values if they learn to speak the language and participate in society: if their children attend UK schools; if they go to parents' meetings; if they work in a variety of employments; if they have access to sporting and leisure activities; and if they engage with different forms of communication (newspapers, internet, radio, television, etc.).

Which cultural traditions from a former country might be unacceptable in the UK?
Which UK values might be different from a former country's values?
- Those who come from patriarchal societies might not share the UK's belief in gender equality.
- Many African Anglican churches are unwilling to tolerate gay or lesbian sexual orientations.
- In the UK many people enjoy alcohol, but this is not allowed in some strict Muslim countries.
- Arranged marriages, female circumcision and honour killings may occur in other countries but are contrary to accepted values in the UK.
- Amputations and corporal punishment are accepted as punishments in some countries, but not the UK.

Would religions appreciate a future king becoming 'Defender of Faith'? Which groups might oppose this?
The group most likely to be doubtful about this would be the Church of England, because recent monarchs have been Defender of the Faith and Head of the Church of England; any dilution of this would possibly not be welcome. Other groups might also be doubtful about a 'Defender of Faith' if he was clearly an Anglican with Anglican beliefs and values.

Review and research

Are there adequate channels in the UK for religious minorities to present their views to the authorities?

If Prince Charles does eventually become King and 'Defender of Faith' then this may set up a new channel of communication. However, even without that, religious minorities are increasingly being heard within UK political parties and other institutions. There are more ethnic minority MPs and peers from different religions: in 2009 there were 12 Labour and two Conservative black or Asian MPs; and Baroness Warsi, a Conservative life peer, was named as the UK's most powerful Muslim woman. There are also no barriers to ethnic minorities participating in the activities of the communications industry.

Should the UK demand that everyone living here always obeys UK law even if it challenges some of their cultural traditions?

If possible, laws should take account of any particular sensitivities within a group or community in the UK, but no-one can be above (or beyond) the law. An example of an exemption in UK law is that rules requiring the compulsory wearing of safety helmets for motorcyclists or those on a building site are waived for Sikhs who wish to wear a turban instead.

Should UK law do more to accommodate the cultural values of UK citizens?

As a general rule, laws involve prohibitions of things – not harming others, not stealing, not damaging property, not discriminating against people or stirring up hatred, not exceeding speed limits when driving, etc. Apart from these restrictions, people are free to choose their own lifestyle. What would not be acceptable would be for people to claim their religion allowed them, for example, to have several wives (breaking laws on monogamy) or to do anything else which the law explicitly forbids.

What happens if different 'rights' conflict?

Lesson objectives	Specification link: Unit 1, Theme 1
By the end of this spread the student should: • understand how freedom of speech can conflict with the right to privacy • understand how freedom of movement can clash with the right to work • understand how other 'rights' may similarly conflict	

Focus

Make sure your students understand concepts such as empathy and fairness. Usually one person's right to freedom of speech or expression is a challenge to someone else's right to privacy. Keep asking students, 'What would be the fair thing to do?' or 'How would you feel if…?'

Key terms

• censorship

• defamation (libel and slander)

• freedom of speech and expression

• freedom of movement

• right of privacy

• right to work

Linked activity sheets

• Heart transplant

• Individuals and change

Starter	Get the students thinking about privacy – for example, if you needed to attend a drug rehabilitation clinic, should the popular press be able to print pictures or report that you were there? Should the same rules apply to 'celebrities' as apply to the rest of us?
Development	Move on to considering freedom of speech and expression. Brainstorm whether there should be any limits on this. Students might briefly refer to defamation, censorship/national security but remember the lesson is about *free speech v privacy*.
	Explain the *freedom of movement versus the right to work* dilemma. Are there some jobs unemployed UK workers don't even apply for? What if workers from other countries work harder or do the job better? If some UK citizens want to go and work in Europe, why shouldn't other European workers come and work here?
	See if students can think of other 'rights' that clash, e.g. the right to a fair trial and the need to keep people safe (detention without charge for up to 28 days).
	Instigate a discussion over the case of Ali and Mohammed Safi – they and their friends hijacked a plane but were acting for fear of their lives. During the hijacking they did effectively imprison the other passengers. Were the UK judges right to say they could not be returned to Afghanistan because they might be subjected to inhuman or degrading treatment or torture?

Plenary	Go over the *Checklist* points. Students could work on the *Further issues* questions as research or homework. Alternatively, they could consider how a fair balance needs to be found when 'rights' conflict – the passengers on the plane were inconvenienced by the hijacking but perhaps the danger to them was far less than the situation from which the hijackers were fleeing.

Answers to questions in the Student Book

What's the issue?

Is it right to limit publicity given to children while still at school?
- Nobody wants to limit publicity given to children who do outstanding things and deserve praise.
- But the children of famous parents deserve to be allowed to grow up like other children, without getting photographed or having their privacy infringed.
- If they get into trouble at school or are involved in sports accidents, why should such actions be publicised when the same does not apply to other children?

Does the general public have the right to know about famous people's private lives?
- It is suggested that, if famous people behave hypocritically, the media and others are entitled to expose them, e.g. if a famous person made lots of statements about the need for fidelity in marriage and was then found to be conducting an adulterous affair.
- In the words of the lawyers, any reports about this might be regarded as 'fair comment on a matter of public interest.
- But human rights laws give everyone the right to privacy and family life.
- Increasingly, the view is being accepted that a sportsperson should be judged for their sporting record or a politician for their political record, and that their family life is no one else's business.

Margin questions

What jobs do you think people from overseas might be willing to do in the UK which UK citizens seem unwilling to do?
- It is often the low-paid jobs involving repetitive, dirty tasks (cleaning fish, picking fruit, cutting and packing vegetables, street sweeping, factory cleaning, etc.). Also, these are sometimes conducted at anti-social times of the day. When the government restricted the number of foreign fruit pickers allowed to come into the country to pick fruit in 2008, much fruit remained unpicked because UK workers could not be recruited to do the work.
- The UK now has a scheme where economic migrants are allowed to come into the country to work only if they have 'shortage' skills to offer, i.e. where there are not enough workers with such skills in the UK labour market.

Was the judge right to rule that the hijackers should remain in the UK? What are the arguments for and against?
The hijackers were fearful for their lives and therefore resorted to extreme measures to get themselves away from Afghanistan. Everyone has the right to life and it is human nature to do one's best to get out of danger. Because the hijackers feared harm (or even death) would come to them if they were returned to Afghanistan, the Court recognised their Article 3 rights. It might be more acceptable to UK citizens if such people (and asylum seekers generally) were allowed to work, earn wages and pay taxes while in the UK, instead of having to live off benefits provided by UK taxpayers.

Review and research

Does it matter that different 'rights' conflict?
It is better that people have rights – even if situations sometimes arise where rights 'conflict' – than that we live in a society where rights are not guaranteed. It is important to remember that, wherever there are rights, there are also responsibilities (as the Natallie Evans/Howard Johnston case demonstrated).

CITIZENSHIP STUDIES

Is any limitation on freedom of speech and expression ever justifiable?

- If a newspaper or an individual makes false or damaging claims against someone, the person can bring a (civil) case for defamation (libel or slander) against them. Substantial damages may be awarded against the newspaper or individual.
- Newspapers and broadcasters are sometimes asked not to publicise particular actions or events as part of a news blackout, e.g. in the case of kidnappings or security threats.
- If journalists become aware of state secrets, it would be damaging to the nation's security for them to become more widely known, so Defence Advisory (DA) Notices are issued; these are a form of censorship.
- It is increasingly recognised that people have the right to privacy, and this has been upheld in a growing list of court cases, so freely expressing information, views or opinions about another person's activities is becoming less acceptable.

Should UK law 'protect' terrorists and hijackers?

- Everyone is entitled to their rights as citizens and human beings.
- We have to be careful before we attach labels to people that may stigmatise them or obscure the truth.
- We need to keep asking what the person did and why they did it.
- If someone has done wrong, they may have to be punished for it and society will wish to prevent them committing similar wrongs again, but that is no reason to deny them their basic rights.
- To do any less would compromise and impoverish the values of society as a whole.

Media – representation and reality:
Media representations

Lesson objectives	Specification link: Unit 1, Theme 2
By the end of this spread the student should: • be able to identify facts, opinion and bias in different media sources • recognise similarities and differences between broadcast and print media and ICT • understand the importance of empathy in helping to develop our opinions	

Focus

...on both the essential media knowledge but also on skills – understanding about facts, opinions and bias and recognising that, if we come to empathise with someone, we may well change our ideas about the circumstances in which they are involved.

Key terms

• bias

• empathy

• media

• popular and quality newspapers

• soaps

• terrestrial

• Internet blogs

Linked activity sheets

• Big Brother is watching you!

• The power of the media

• How much hinges on a headline?

Starter	Start off with a current news story – perhaps from a local paper – and get students to consider that a media representation may sometimes not tell the whole story or totally reflect reality.
Development	Then let them look at a newspaper report in which there are both facts and opinions. Explain that a fact is supported by evidence and can be verified, while an opinion is sometimes belief (it reflects their values), and not everyone will agree. Ask the students to practise identifying facts and opinions.
	Then consider bias. In popular papers, editors' opinions are often clear throughout the story – they emphasise their point of view. Sometimes bias occurs by omitting some facts or parts of a story. Sometimes a newspaper that strongly favours one party never mentions other parties except to criticise them. It will be easy to find bias on Internet blogs since no one expects them to be impartial.
	Leave plenty of time to explore the idea of 'empathy'. It may be appropriate to refer to someone who people in the class know and like – perhaps a person with a disability – so the question could be 'how would you feel if you were in the same position as...?' Many of them will identify with characters and their escapades in *Emmerdale* or *Hollyoaks*. A gay, lesbian or ethnic minority soap character they like may help change any negative attitudes they have towards

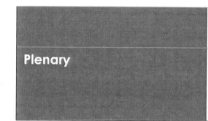

CITIZENSHIP STUDIES

	other gay or lesbian or ethnic minority people. Empathy is an excellent means of challenging discrimination.
Plenary	Go over the *Checklist* points. The students could work on the *Further issues* questions as research or homework. Or you may want them to think about how empathising with someone might change their point of view.

Answers to questions in the Student Book

What's the issue?

Is *The Sun*'s headline a fact? What is the headline trying to do?
- Of course Dr John Reid's brain isn't missing – but this is typical of the joke headlines popular papers often have.
- *The Sun* is humorously pointing out its disagreement with Dr Reid over a policy issue.

Compare the front pages. What are the differences and similarities?
- In the past the size of pages of popular newspapers was different from those of quality papers – that is why we used to refer to quality papers as 'broadsheets' and popular papers as 'tabloids'.
- Even now *The Daily Telegraph* and *The Guardian* have bigger page sizes than *The Independent* or *The Times*, whose pages are now the same size as popular papers such as *The Daily Mirror* or *The Sun*.
- Generally, quality papers have more serious headlines – as in *The Independent*'s headline and graphic, which highlight how isolated the UK and US were in opposing a Middle East ceasefire.
- Quality papers are more likely to have eye-catching photographs or graphics than previously but the biggest difference is that they are less likely than popular papers to mix up factual news coverage with the newspaper's own opinions (i.e. the opinions of the editor or owner).

Why are newspapers and Internet blogs more biased than radio or television?
There is no expectation or requirement that newspapers or Internet blogs should be impartial. Terrestrial broadcasters in the UK (BBC and ITV) are required by UK law to offer balanced and impartial programmes – any strong opinion included needs to be balanced by a different opinion from someone else. Some satellite broadcasters, such as Fox News, are just as biased as the most biased newspapers or Internet blogs.

Margin questions

Which newspapers give the clearest idea of the news – popular or quality?
- Popular newspapers recognise that many people buy them for sport, news of celebrities, horoscopes, competitions, cartoons and entertainment – serious news is not as high up their priorities as it is for quality papers.
- Most people who buy quality papers do so because they want to be kept up to date with serious news.

What does the Office of Communications do? How effective is it? How powerful is it?
- Ofcom is a department that regulates broadcasters, making sure they stick to the Broadcasting Codes. They have significant power and effectiveness and are readily able to control broadcasters and handle complaints.

Review and research

Do we buy newspapers for news or for entertainment?
Probably both. Many people who want to keep abreast of serious news in quality papers will also enjoy the lifestyle features or competitions or free entertainment dvds also offered. The proportion of serious news and the extent of comprehensive news coverage are much greater in quality than in popular papers.

How has the wider use of the Internet affected newspapers and broadcasters?
- Newspaper sales are declining because people can access news in many different ways. BBC news broadcasts can be seen on people's mobiles or via the Internet.

- Also whereas people used to look at one newspaper with one political point of view (e.g. *The Daily Telegraph* –Conservative or *The Guardian* – Labour/Lib Dem), the Internet allows them to view the content of different papers, so the influence of papers is lessened.

How can soaps affect people's opinions on key moral issues such as discrimination and abortion?

- Soaps are closely followed by millions – characters become almost like family members to viewers, and people often identify with particular characters.
- People who dislike gay men or women may warm to a gay character in a soap opera and soften their general opinions as a result.
- A person who feels too many people from ethnic minorities have settled in the UK may empathise with an ethnic minority character and feel it would be unfair or unreasonable for the character to be deported.
- Soaps help us see the human side of many policy issues and, as we empathise with particular characters in specific situations, they may cause us to shift our general point of view.
- People with strong views about abortion may feel less certain when a favourite character is struggling to make a decision about an unwanted pregnancy.

CITIZENSHIP STUDIES

Issues and news agendas

Lesson objectives	Specification link: Unit 1, Theme 2
By the end of this spread the student should: • understand how and the extent to which the media reflect, distort or create opinion • recognise the ways in which different forms of media are regulated	

Focus

...on the limitations on media freedom – they can be constrained by DA notices (a form of censorship), laws of defamation, people's rights of privacy, rulings of the Press Complaints Commission (PCC) and Ofcom. Make sure your students are very clear that Ofcom is much more powerful than the PCC – and why.

Key terms

- censorship
- defamation – libel and slander
- Liberty – pressure group
- moral panics and folk devils
- OFCOM

- Mosquito
- privacy
- respect
- Youth Parliament
- PCC

Linked activity sheets

- Launch your own pressure group
- How much hinges on a headline?

Starter	Begin by discussing the Mosquito device. Have students come across them? Why would shopkeepers and newspapers think they were a good idea? What opposition did they attract? Why did some newspapers change their mind?
Development	Then look at newspapers – if possible, provide several papers for the same day to show how similar news stories are approached from different angles. Also, point out how what is big news in one paper may be hardly mentioned in another. Examples are given of 'typical' newspaper viewpoints. Can the students think of others?
	Papers often demonise certain individuals or groups to make them seem hate figures or folk devils (e.g. hoodies or paedophiles), although it is understandable why some individuals may be hated for doing or saying despicable things.
	But there is a danger of stereotyping – not all Muslims are terrorists: the vast majority are friendly, law-abiding people.
	Most teenagers would never dream of knifing people – most are friendly and only a few get involved in knife crime.
	Newspapers who wind up their readers with perhaps exaggerated fears are said to be creating a 'moral panic'. Work through the *Regulating the media* section – distinguish between censorship (e.g. for reasons of national security), defamation (unfairly attacking

CITIZENSHIP STUDIES

	someone's reputation), infringing a person's right to privacy, and the difference between the PCC and Ofcom.
Plenary	Go over the *Checklist* points. Students can work on the *Further issues* questions as research or homework. Or you may want them to think about whether the media need to be regulated more fully. An apology after a complaint never has as much impact as the original statements that gave offence.

Answers to questions in the Student Book

What's the issue?

How have public views about the issue changed?
- Originally the Mosquito was seen as a useful device to stop youngsters gathering in particular parts of town centres and to force them to move on.
- Some people saw a large group of youngsters as threatening and some traders thought their presence reduced their trade or increased shoplifting.
- But most of the youngsters who were moved on were normal, unthreatening teenagers.
- The high-pitched noise was essentially anti-social and increasingly seen as something society should not inflict on anyone. If people with disabilities or from ethnic minorities were discriminated against in this way there would rightly be an outcry.
- As pressure groups and young people in the Youth Parliament became vocal in opposing the Mosquito, the tide of opinion moved from being heavily in favour, to being more sceptical, and then to downright opposition.

How important are pressure groups for changing opinions and decisions?
- Sometimes existing bodies such as a church or a sports club or business may take a stand for or against a proposal and become almost 'temporary pressure groups'.
- Sometimes pressure groups campaign for certain issues – trade unions demanding higher pay or better working conditions; environmental groups opposing destruction of rain forests or excessive carbon emissions leading to global warming or climate change; motoring groups calling for reduced taxes on fuel.
- They are important because individuals work together through pressure groups to achieve changes they seek. The government is always particularly interested in the technical advice and expertise they receive from groups such as the NFU (farmers), Age Concern (elderly) or Shelter (homeless).
- Groups that find the government does not share their point of view may engage in publicity-seeking stunts – these may not yield an immediate result in terms of changed policies but may lead to shifts in public opinion in the long term, e.g. Fathers4Justice (rights of fathers) or Plane Stupid (dangers of aircraft emissions).

Why does Kent County Council now want the Mosquito banned?
Kent County Council, which originally thought the Mosquito to be socially useful has now come to recognise that it discriminates against young people, demonstrating that pressure group campaigns and lobbying by young people have worked.

Margin questions

Why have views changed about using the Mosquito to move young people on from parks or shopping areas?
Every young person moved on is someone's son or daughter. At a time when young people are taught the importance of 'respect' it is clear the Mosquito was sending out the very opposite message, hence the change in attitude.

How important do you think newspapers, the Internet or broadcasts were in causing the change?
Young people bombarded the Internet and broadcasters with their views – proving that young people can make a difference. In the end *The Daily Mail* came round to backing the removal of the Mosquito in many public areas but Internet pressure was probably the most significant cause of the change in opinion.

Review and research

Are the media more interested in telling the truth or making profits?

The terrestrial broadcasters are bound to tell the truth and to apologise and issue corrections if they make a mistake. They are closely regulated by Ofcom. Newspapers and the Internet have greater freedom and are certainly interested in making profits from advertising, so anything that increases readership or the numbers visiting a website is likely to improve profitability. Newspapers are less regulated than terrestrial radio and television (since the PCC is an example of an industry regulating itself), but in their reporting they are still subject to laws of libel (if they damage people's reputation unfairly) and must not breach a individuals' human rights – particularly their right to privacy.

Can the media influence opinion in elections?

- Most newspapers make their recommendations to readers very clear as an election approaches. People often buy a particular paper because they share its point of view. Most *Daily Telegraph* readers are Conservative, most *Guardian* readers are Labour or Liberal Democrat supporters, so the readers will probably be unsurprised by a recommendation.
- However, the biggest circulation popular newspaper, *The Sun*, supported the Conservatives before 1997 when it switched support to Labour – and it might back the Conservatives in future.
- The people most likely to be influenced by a newspaper are those who buy a paper for other reasons – sport, celebrity news, etc. – and are carried along by its treatment of political stories as the election day approaches.

Do codes of practice and laws relating to the media give individuals strong enough rights to complain?

- Both Ofcom (with their Broadcasting Code) and the PCC give clear rights for people to complain.
- Look at the websites of both organisations for examples of recent cases over which they have issued adjudications.
- Whether such rights are strong enough is debatable: a press story about which people make complaints often gains bigger headlines and more column inches than any apology or correction buried deep on an inside page in small print.

Information is power:
Public debate and policy formation

Lesson objectives	Specification link: Unit 1, Theme 2

By the end of this spread the student should:

• understand how politicians use the media to communicate with the public

• recognise the extent of bias in the media

Focus

...on the idea 'information is power' – if you don't know about a proposal, you have no reason to protest. That is why consultations are so important. How individuals respond to consultations can be strongly influenced by the media, just as how they vote in elections can also be influenced.

Key terms

• consultations

• eco-town

• impartiality

• mobilising consent

• general election

• Labour Party

• Conservative Party

• Liberal Democrat Party

Starter	Has a school/college policy that was discussed in the School Council changed recently (uniform, sports played, food)? If students weren't been told about an idea in advance, they couldn't offer suggestions or comments before a final decision was taken. Have students discuss issues of fairness and repression.
Development	From *What's the issue?* ask students to think of areas in a town or village where new building has taken place – how would neighbours have felt if they had not known about plans in advance? Neighbours are usually consulted by the planning department of the local council so people can offer comments if they wish. How much notice should be taken of the opposition of neighbours?
	Nationally, governments publish Green Papers on key issues for consultation – people can offer their ideas by writing letters or commenting on government websites.
	Think about consultation. Even if people don't agree, they are more likely to accept a decision if they have had their say. Ample consultation in advance gives a better chance of people obeying laws even if they don't agree with them – e.g. 'mobilising consent' for changing speed limits.
	Politicians' and parties' reputations depend largely on how they are represented in the media – and these representations may depend on the views of the newspaper's owner or editor. In April 2009 most Conservative-leaning newspapers criticised Alistair Darling, the Chancellor of the Exchequer, for his budget proposals but the Labour-leaning *Daily Mirror* supported both Darling and his budget. The same can happen to candidates and parties in elections. Look at spending figures for parties in elections – does it matter if some parties have a lot more to spend than others?

CITIZENSHIP STUDIES

Plenary	Go over the *Checklist* points. Students could work on the *Further issues* questions as research or homework. Or you may want them to spend some time exploring the 10 Downing St website.

Answers to questions in the Student Book

What's the issue?

How can it be claimed that 'information is power'?
- If people do not know about a proposal to build on a field, they will not make a case opposing it.
- So the very knowledge of a proposal empowers individuals to influence the final decision.
- It is now recognised that all planning decisions should be advertised beforehand so affected individuals or organisations can put their representations forward.
- Some people feel that opponents for large-scale schemes (new roads, power stations, airport runways) are given too many opportunities to slow things down and there has been talk of fast-tracking procedures to reduce delay.
- It is important for everyone to know about proposals in advance and for their views to be taken fully into account before a final decision is made.

What are the arguments for and against secrecy?
- People wanting to avoid public debate or having particular proposals subjected to close public scrutiny will prefer secrecy but this is wholly contrary to the values of modern society.
- The public believes information should be freely available unless there are very strong reasons for keeping some matters confidential (e.g. personal matters concerning individuals, affecting no one but themselves).
- The human right to privacy is the justification for keeping personal information secret.
- However, for matters involving society as a whole, a general concern for greater openness led to the Freedom of Information Act being passed in 2000 – a powerful blow to secrecy.

How can the media help those who support or oppose particular proposals?
- By giving publicity to campaigns for or against a particular proposal, the media can ensure that a controversial idea is not accepted with insufficient debate or consideration.
- The media may report protests or demonstrations and will often devote time or space to giving information about exactly what is proposed, why some people support it and why some oppose it.

Margin questions

How widely do people have access to the media? Are there some people who are left out? Does this matter?
Most people have access to radio or television, many see newspapers and increasing numbers have access to the Internet, but inevitably there are some who do not have access to these news sources either because they cannot afford to or because they cannot or do not wish to be involved. In a free democratic society, everyone needs information and it does matter if some people become socially excluded. Those who cannot read or write, the homeless and people with disabilities can easily be left out. This is why recent governments have placed great emphasis on eliminating the social exclusion of a whole underclass of individuals.

Why do you think there is such a big difference in the amounts spent by different political parties? Is there a case for political parties to get their funding from the state?
- The Labour Party has traditionally received much funding from trade unions but, as trade union membership has declined, providing such funding has sometimes become more difficult.
- The Conservatives have depended on wealthy individuals and the fund-raising activities of Conservative Associations to produce enormous amounts of funding to try to win seats in Parliament from other parties.
- Some people believe that parties are too influenced by their financial supporters, and that Labour would be better off if it didn't depend on trade union funds and the Conservatives on similar funding from business and wealthy individuals.
- The Liberal Democrats do not have major sources of funding on which they can rely, so probably depend more than the other parties on funds given or raised by its members.

CITIZENSHIP STUDIES

- The case for state funding of political parties is that it would give vested interests less influence over political parties.
- Those in favour say no one should be able to 'buy' influence and that democracy is too important to be taken for granted.

See also the Electoral Commission website (http://www.electoralcommission.org.uk/).

Review and research

Should governments do what they think is right or should they try to take into account the pressure from media sources and groups?

If a government did not do what it considered right, it surely wouldn't consider doing things it knew were 'wrong'. Some people see decision-making as a tug-of-war – but if one side of an argument has massive resources to publicise its case, it would be unfair if it 'won' because others lacked matching resources. When new towns like Milton Keynes were proposed, many people bitterly opposed their creation – yet most people now find them perfectly acceptable, so opposition to change (e.g. building eco-towns) should not be rejected purely because the idea has attracted opposition. The people who need new housing to live in probably have fewer resources for campaigning than those who want to resist change. Government has to look at its long-term objectives, take people's concerns seriously but in the end do what it considers to be right.

Is it a good thing that there are such big differences in party political spending during elections and can this be controlled?

- Candidates and political parties must supply information on donations and expenditure to the Electoral Commission; they must also stick to expenditure limits enforced by the Commission.
- The fact that parties do not have equal resources is seen by some as an argument in favour of state funding so that an election is fought on a level playing field.
- Others say that far too much publicity is produced at election times and that the levels of permitted expenditure should be greatly reduced.

CITIZENSHIP STUDIES

Influencing public opinion

Lesson objectives	Specification link: Unit 1, Theme 2
By the end of this spread the student should: • understand how the media are used to influence public opinion and those in power • recognise the role and importance of opinion polls	

Focus

...on whether people buy newspapers because they know the paper looks at issues in the same way as they do or whether they decide on the paper they buy for other reasons and may be influenced by the opinion expressed.

Key terms

- advertising
- civil servant
- opinion leader
- opinion poll

- public opinion
- trade union
- policy

Linked activity sheets

- Launch your own pressure group
- Big Brother is watching you
- The power of the media
- The great biscuit election

Starter	Why do nearly 10 times more people buy *The Sun* than *The Guardian*? Which of the newspapers listed are quality papers and which are popular papers?
Development	Focus on why people buy papers –sports stories, cartoons, pictures, horoscopes, 'jokey' news stories, celebrity gossip – few people buy them for in-depth coverage of the news and politics.
	But newspapers still influence those who buy them for other reasons. The paper may encourage people to watch one TV programme rather than another. The adverts may mean people choose one shop over another. Even if few people buy papers for political reasons, many may be influenced by what they say.
	Detailed comments on policy are most likely to appear in quality papers read by civil servants and politicians – so letters to newspapers about a policy could be seen by civil servants or ministers working on the final version of the policy.
	Newspapers are not the only influences. We can be influenced by other forms of media – radio, television and Internet.
	Often our decisions follow our basic values learned from parents, teachers or by belonging to bodies such as trade unions - if a newspaper's view opposes these values, we are less likely to adopt its point of view.

CITIZENSHIP STUDIES

	How do we measure public opinion? Polls. Ask students to think about their reliability. How would you construct a 5% sample of school students on an issue? What sample would be most likely to give the most reliable result? How can opinion polls influence how we behave?
Plenary	Go over the *Checklist* points. Students could work on the *Further issues* questions as research or homework. Or they could consider how and why public opinion changes – e.g. why support for different political parties or leaders fluctuates.

Answers to questions in the Student Book

What's the issue?

Which newspapers have most impact on public opinion: the popular papers that most people read or the quality papers that fewer people read, which go into things in greater detail?
- Big headlines with instant judgements in popular papers may cause short-term swings in public opinion as measured by the polls.
- Sometimes popular papers try to demonise particular individuals or cause moral panics over certain groups (hoodies, economic migrants, asylum seekers), based largely on prejudice.
- Elections involve a range of issues so a campaign by a popular paper over one particular issue may not have much effect on an election outcome.
- Arguably quality papers with much smaller readerships have a greater impact on public opinion because many of their readers are opinion leaders with influence in their communities; such opinions are backed up by more hard reasoning than usually appears in the popular press.

As newspaper sales fall, which media source has the biggest influence on how we think and what we do?
- More people rely on televison and radio for their news than on the Internet.
- Increasing numbers of people give personal feedback to blogs on the Internet and the websites of terrestrial broadcasters and thus contribute to the making of public opinion.
- A problem is that, as newspaper sales fall, some people may become less engaged by issues in the news.
- This is bad because democracy depends on engagement and their and making choices between parties at elections, reflecting their different policies for the future and – significantly – assessing a party's record of achievement in the past.
- More people now focus on things that matter to them by joining and campaigning through pressure groups but these are very partial bodies – if people do not keep an impartial eye on events, the policy preferences they choose may be out of step with events or changing circumstances.

Why are popular papers much cheaper than quality ones?
Large parts of the costs of production of a newspaper are met by advertising. If *The Sun* is likely to be purchased by nearly 3 million people, it will be more attractive to advertisers than *The Guardian* or *The Independent*, so such papers will either attract less advertising or be able to charge less for space in their paper. For that reason the price of *The Guardian* or *The Independent* is always likely to be significantly higher than mass circulation popular papers.

Margin questions

Radio and television programmes are supposed to be less biased than newspapers because they don't just put forward one point of view. Does it help you make up your mind if you hear more than one point of view expressed?
Hearing different points of view, supported by various arguments, makes it easier to get to grips with an issue – this is what comes out of a discussion on radio or television. Newspapers and individual Internet blogs are likely to offer one point of view that may be less objective and, in the absence of the cut and thrust of debate, individuals may find greater difficulty in deciding whether or not they agree.

CITIZENSHIP STUDIES

Review and research

Should newspapers and the Internet be made to avoid bias, as broadcasters are?

- The advantage of the press in the UK is that it is free (taking into account that some would disagree).
- People, including newspaper editors, their reporters and columnists, can say what they want and readers can decide whether or not they agree.
- If bias was avoided, there might be no debate over issues and policies for the future – this starts to resemble the situation in undemocratic one-party states.
- Greater objectivity in newspapers might be achieved if, rather than having to eliminate bias, they were encouraged to give both sides of an argument and thus replicate the balanced coverage achieved by terrestrial broadcast media.

Which types of newspapers have the biggest impact on public opinion?

- Popular papers with large readerships can often swing large numbers of their readers to support a particular view in the short term.
- Quality papers are more likely to be read by decision-makers and opinion leaders and many people will become engaged with issues through reading them, though they may not always agree.

How do opinion polls assist policy making and democracy?

- General elections are held about every four years so, between such contests, opinion polls provide the best guide to movements in public opinion.
- Opinion polls are invaluable to decision-makers: they reflect people's views of affairs and what needs to be done – decision-makers will often test out possible policies by commissioning private opinion polls.
- In elections opinion polls often help voters decide which parties have a chance of winning in a particular constituency – in Worcester, the main battle is between Labour and the Conservatives, so many Liberal Democrats may choose to vote for one of the other two parties if they want their vote to make a difference but in nearby Hereford the battle is mainly between Liberal Democrats and Conservatives with Labour in third place, so many Labour supporters may vote Liberal Democrat or Conservative if they want to make a difference. This is known as tactical voting.
- During the hunting debate, the Countryside Alliance emphasised the support shown in opinion polls to try to suggest that MPs would be behaving undemocratically if they went against public opinion on the issue.

In particular

Since the student book was written, *The Daily Telegraph* (a quality newspaper that hadn't campaigned in this way before) published in May 2009 astonishing expenses claims made by MPs, resulting in big sums of money being repaid and some resignations. It was said that many people ceased to trust MPs as a result. A succession of daily revelations, repeated in the other media, horrified the public (as the opinion polls showed), caused Mr Speaker Michael Martin to resign and seemed to cause many voters to abstain or to switch their support away from Labour.

Law and society:
Crime: rising or falling?

Lesson objectives	Specification link: Unit 1, Theme 2
By the end of this spread the student should: • understand the different levels of crime in the UK and general trends • recognise the impact crime has on society and the problems in measuring crime • be aware of the relationships between crime, conscience, law and morality	

Focus

...on problems of measuring crime (different figures from police statistics and British Crime Survey), recognise that overall crime has fallen in recent years (though sometimes the media seem to try to create a moral panic over knife crime, which has increased) and also focus on the ethical aspects of law, morality and conscience in relation to abortion, assisted suicide and euthanasia.

Key terms

• British Crime Survey

• conscience and morality

• Crown Prosecution Service

• euthanasia

• fraud and forgery

• households

• Social Trends

• police statistics

Linked activity sheets

• Reducing the potential for crime in your area

• Victimless crimes?

• Crime

• What do you think about the law?

Starter	Look at the latest edition of Social Trends issued each year (39 was issued in April 2009) for the latest trends. Throw questions at the students to give them a chance to express their perceptions of crime – has it risen or fallen, who fears it most, who is most likely to be a victim, etc? Social Trends 39 reports BCS's finding that crime fell in England & Wales from 19m offences in 1995 to 10m offences in 2007/8.
Development	Then use the list of crimes to relate the stats to their perceptions. Emphasise that the stats may be incomplete because some crimes will not be reported for the reasons stated – consider why people might not report crime. Why do the elderly fear crime most when in fact the young are most likely to be victims? Is this because elderly people generally feel more vulnerable (mention empathy here)? Or perhaps they are frightened by media exaggerations? Consider the law and morality question – because something is immoral it may not be unlawful: telling lies and committing adultery are immoral but neither is illegal

CITIZENSHIP STU

	in the UK. Citizenship gives rights and responsibilities to individuals – it does not expect everyone to feel the same about things. Some MPs would like to make abortions harder to obtain (believing a foetus is a life), others believe women must have the right to choose and determine what happens in their own bodies. Does an anti-abortion campaigner have the right to dictate to someone who may feel his/her different values just as firmly? Or is it right for Parliament to try to do so? Similar issues arise over euthanasia, assisted suicide and whether sick individuals can or should have medical interventions forced on them.
Plenary	Go over the *Checklist* points. Students could work on the *Further issues* questions as research or homework. You could ask them to speculate on how crime figures in their area might be similar to or different from national stats and then give them the task of finding the actual figures.

Answers to questions in the Student Book

What's the issue?

Why do people commit crime?
The particular reasons will differ according to the crime – the reasons for using illegal drugs or committing sexual offences will not be the same as those for motoring offences or committing theft or violence against a person. Much theft arises because the thieves want money to fund a drug habit. People who commit crime haven't been socialised to behave as good citizens and seem to have got the balance between rights and responsibilities wrong – they probably don't accept that everyone has a responsibility to behave honestly and to obey laws.

Why are young people most often victims of crime?
Very often young people rent accommodation with others and may find it difficult to keep their property safe. If they have a car, it may be parked on the street, making it easier to steal the vehicle or to steal from it. Many young people socialise at night and can be caught up in fights or violence.

Can crime ever be justified?
In a word, no. A person who shoplifts may have run out of money but in welfare state Britain there is no need for anyone to be destitute. A person who drives dangerously can do serious harm to others. A person who takes property from someone's house may destroy the occupants' sense of security at home. Sometimes a person found guilty of crime may need to be treated with special consideration if there are particular circumstances such as having a mental health condition or acting to get a sick person to hospital – but that does not make the crime itself any more acceptable.

Margin questions

Do you think that fewer crimes would be committed if the punishments were more severe?
Some people - including some judges - favour heavy sentences to put the offender and others off the idea of committing further crime. This is the idea of setting up deterrents to crime. As you will see on later pages, over 70% of offenders are never apprehended, which means many criminals have good reason to believe they won't suffer a heavy penalty because they are unlikely to get caught. In Citizenship it's important to understand that laws should be obeyed because it's right to do so and not because the potentially guilty person wants to avoid punishment. If we don't like a law we should campaign in democratic ways to change it, not just break it because it suits us to do so. Some people say different punishments should be used. Would young people guilty of vandalism or antisocial behaviour be more likely to behave if they thought they could lose their driving licence or be evicted from the house in which they lived? Perhaps - but it's worth remembering that countries with much more severe punishments than the UK (China and the USA with the death penalty, Singapore and Malaysia with corporal punishment) do not have noticeably lower crime levels than the UK. Whatever happens, it is important to treat everyone with respect - humiliating offenders is unlikely to improve their behaviour.

Is the real problem that too many people have not learned that committing crime (breaking the law) is wrong and can never be right, whatever excuses are offered?

If people treat others in the ways they themselves would like to be treated, more consideration would be evident in society. Some people claim that young people have become less aware of right and wrong and the accompanying moral boundaries as a result of so many households now being headed by a single, working parent – especially since moral boundaries that traditionally came from the churches are less respected in today's more secular society. Perhaps that is why Citizenship is now part of the national curriculum – to help redress the balance.

There has recently been lots of concern about knife crime. Is this a real problem, or have the media exaggerated it?

In May 2008 *The Independent* asked whether knife crime was out of control. They reported the following answers:

Yes...

- The murder of 15 London teenagers in just five months emphasizes the extent of the problem
- Hospitals report they are treating growing numbers of patients with serious wounds
- If only four percent of young people sometimes carry knives, thousands of blades are on the streets

No...

- Violent knife attacks remain statistically very rare events in Britain. We shouldn't worry about such an attack
- The numbers of knife assaults appear to have remained stable over the last decade
- Knife crime is mainly concentrated in a small number of the largest cities and in particular areas of those cities

Is there a case for making euthanasia or assisted suicide (helping to kill someone who has an incurable illness or injury, with that person's consent) legal in the UK? Or is human life so sacred that everything possible should always be done to preserve life?

Such questions are probably the most difficult to decide. Current medicine is now much more successful than previously and provides hope to many – but when the possibilities of having a quality lifestyle seem to have run out, significant numbers of people look to assisted suicide. Such decisions depend heavily on morality and conscience. The UK does sometimes change the law on such questions. Up until the 1960s people who unsuccessfully attempted suicide could be (and were) sent to prison. In a country that now allows gay and lesbian couples to engage in civil partnerships, it is worth remembering that homosexual activity was unlawful up until the middle of the last century. Abortion and assisted suicide are the two most hotly debated moral questions at present. The law needs to reflect the moral standards of society as a whole. But has society really moved such boundaries enough for Parliament to be justified in changing the law? More people campaigning for change does not mean that it is the right step to take.

Be on the lookout:

For information about Crime Partnerships in your area. These are alliances between business and police, which aim to reduce crime.

Review and research

Which measure of crime should you believe – police statistics or the British Crime Survey?

Comparing police statistics year on year gives a clear idea of trends. The same is true of the British Crime Survey (BCS). Look again at the reasons why some crimes are not reported to the police – such crimes largely make up the difference between police statistics and BCS statistics. One argument sometimes advanced is that police statistics reflect the crimes that are serious enough for people to report. BCS data is the result of surveys completed by a tiny minority of people, which are then extrapolated to suggest figures for the whole population. It is a useful guide but probably more of an approximation than the police statistics published. Get the students to consider whether or when they would report a crime

Do the media exaggerate fear of crime?

- The media make headlines out of crime – as a good way to sell newspapers – yet since 1995 BCS crime figures have almost halved.
- The fear caused by crime figures is a good example of the media creating a moral panic which may be unjustified by the reality.

CITIZENSHIP STUDIES

Do today's laws match up with the moral values we hold in a modern society?

- Trying to keep the law in line with prevailing moral values has been the cause of many changes in the law over the years, resulting in the end of capital and corporal punishment, easier divorce and abortion, the acceptance of gay and lesbian lifestyles and the decriminalising of suicide.
- Above we saw there is pressure to allow assisted suicide and some people argue in favour of decriminalising cannabis use, but abortion campaigners are currently seeking to reverse contemporary trends and make abortion more difficult to obtain.

CITIZENSHIP STUDIES

Reducing crime

Lesson objectives	Specification link: Unit 1, Theme 2
By the end of this spread the student should: • understand that most offenders are not detected, though figures vary between different crimes • recognise the role of the Youth Offending Teams • know how the National Probation Service supports offenders, victims and society	

Focus

...on reasons for some detection rates being so low and how this could affect the attitudes of criminals. Also concentrate on the relative effectiveness of community punishments as opposed to prison.

Key terms

• community

• community support officers

• community sentences (or punishments)

• demonstrations

• detection rates

• deterrent

• rehabilitation

• MacPherson report

• police

• probation

• recidivism

• reparation

• terrorism

Linked activity sheets

• Reducing the potential for crime in your area

• Victimless crimes

• Crime

• What do you think about the law?

Starter	Brainstorm the *Key terms* – police, community support officers, Youth Offending Teams, National Probation Service (NPS) – ask students to consider what they do, in what ways they are effective or ineffective.
Development	Focus on detection – why are some rates higher than others? Why might it be difficult to improve some detection rates? Should more citizens report those whom they know are committing crime? Do low detection rates mean that the possibility of punishment is a very weak deterrent? What are the most important roles of the police? Should their priorities be changed? Should they leave motoring offences to community support officers? Would Youth Offending Teams be needed if parents kept a close enough eye on their children? Given the nature of modern society and the work they undertake, the answer is certainly 'yes'.

CITIZENSHIP STUDIES

	Focus on the NPS – why are community punishments apparently more successful than prison in terms of recidivism rates? How does the NPS support communities and victims as well as offenders?
Plenary	Go over the *Checklist* points. Students could work on the *Further issues* questions as research or homework. Or you may want them to find out the crime detection rates in the area where they live or download a crime map for the area (see Directgov website - http://policingpledge.direct.gov.uk/index.html).

Answers to questions in the Student Book

What's the issue?

Why are detection rates much higher for some crimes than for others?
- If someone is found dealing or in possession of illegal drugs, the guilty person is easy to identify and a high detection rate is therefore not surprising.
- Often people will know or be able to positively identify anyone who is violent towards them.
- Similarly many victims of rape or other sexual offences will know their attacker, so detection rates are above average.
- In cases of theft or criminal damage, where the guilty person will often not be known to the victim, it isn't surprising detection rates are lower.

Does society do enough to teach everyone that crime is wrong?
- Attacking or stealing from people is likely to cause them physical or psychological pain.
- That is why Citizenship teaches us we should empathise with others to understand how they feel about things and why they act as they do.
- If selfish people recognised the pain (to which they would not wish to be exposed themselves) that crime causes their victim, they would hopefully be less likely to commit crime.

How could detection rates be increased?
- As police hold more DNA records, it is becoming increasingly possible to detect those responsible for crimes committed years ago.
- Detection rates need police and/or support officers to work on such cases.
- Offenders who commit crime are most likely to be apprehended if crimes are reported quickly and there are enough police officers to work on the case.
- It is often suggested that, if police officers could devote more time to pursuing criminals and less doing routine paperwork, more offenders would be identified.

Margin questions

If parents acted as responsible people keeping their children in order and punishing them if they did bad things, would we need Youth Offending Teams?
Most people agree there is a need in the UK for 'joined-up government'. Youth Offending Teams help to provide this because they bring together representatives of police, probation service, social services, health, education and specialists dealing with drugs/alcohol misuse, all of which can call on resources to which most conscientious parents would never have access. A youngster in trouble may need support from social services if care at home is inadequate or may need to be rehabilitated from drug or alcohol misuse – in conjunction with the school or a doctor.

Review and research

Are criticisms of the police justified?
The 2007/08 British Crime Survey said that 65% of people in England and Wales had overall confidence in the police in their local area, a 1% increase since 2006/07; 83% agreed that the local police would treat them

with respect if they had contact with them and 64% said their local police would treat everyone fairly regardless of who they are, and that they understand the issues affecting their community (62%). People had the least confidence in relying on their local police to deal with minor crimes (43%) – which perhaps helps to explain why many crimes are not reported in the first place.

Do you think community punishments are better than sending offenders to prison?

- Many of the people sent to prison have social problems that may largely explain their crime.
- Punishment in the community tends to reduce reoffending rates and, if an offender has a family and a job, a punishment in the community means that home, family and job links are maintained.
- Based in the community, an offender who needs to be taught to read or write or to gain skills that will make an employer want to give him (or her) a job has a better chance of accessing such support through a local college or similar education outlet.

Should parents be more responsible for the behaviour of their teenage children?

- A big problem is 'absentee parents' who are either working most of the time to keep the home together, or where a child is brought up by just one parent while the other may live with another family elsewhere.
- What teenagers need is not lavish presents but consistent support and clear rules and structures on which they can depend as and when they feel they need to use them.
- Above all, children of all ages need adults to be role models with whom they can identify – if parents do not or cannot do this they may come to admire other people, some of whom may not behave as a responsible role model should.
- In view of the inadequacies discovered in some social services departments, it has been suggested that, instead of putting children with inadequate parental support into care, full-time places should be provided for them in boarding schools.

Courts at work

Lesson objectives	Specification link: Unit 1, Theme 2
By the end of this spread the student should: • know the main courts in England and Wales and who presides over them • recognise the main differences between barristers and solicitors, and the role of juries	

Focus

...on the roles of different people in the courtroom – who does what. Also make sure your students think about how they would feel if they were a juror – would they find someone guilty if they thought the likely punishment was too harsh? Might they find someone guilty because they didn't like how he/she looked or not guilty if they felt some empathy with the person?

Key terms

• barristers and solicitors

• Crown Court

• defence

• judge

• jury

• Kingsnorth Six

• magistrates and district judges

• Supreme Court

• prosecution

Linked activity sheets

• Heart transplant

• Crime

• The UK legal pyramids

Starter	If you are planning to take your students to watch a Magistrates or Crown Court case, this material may be a suitable preparation. Explain that laws are made to protect everyone but punishments of those found guilty can be varied according to circumstances.
Development	The diagram is a reasonable representation of a court, though the one in your area may look slightly different. Outline the different roles. Discuss with the students how they would feel if they were the judge... or the accused... or the media... or the victim... or the accused's relatives in the public gallery... or a member of the defence or prosecution teams (could be either a barrister or solicitor) for whom this may be just another day's work. Then lead a discussion on whether Martin is guilty and what sentence he should get if he is found guilty – check the CPS website for current sentencing practice for dangerous driving. In 2009 the rules were: (i) 2 years' imprisonment or a fine or both if tried in Crown Court but, for a summary conviction in Magistrates Court, imprisonment not exceeding 6 months, or a fine, or both. (ii) In either court 12 months is the minimum period of disqualification from driving, endorsement of driving licence is obligatory together with mandatory disqualification from driving until an extended driving test is passed. (iii) Non-custodial options may be considered, but usually a custodial penalty is appropriate, especially where a number of aggravating factors

	combine. Make sure your students understand the main points about different courts, barristers and solicitors and the role of juries.
Plenary	Go over the *Checklist* points. Students might work on the *Further issues* questions as research or homework. Or they could think about whether there should be fixed penalties that all offenders automatically receive. Or, they could explore how they would act if they were on a jury when someone had broken the law for what they considered a good reason.

Answers to questions in the Student Book

What's the issue?

Is Martin guilty or not guilty?
- Martin was driving at 60mph in a 40mph area and he did knock down and injure the elderly woman who was on the pavement so it is difficult to see how he could be 'not guilty'.
- But what was he guilty of – were the police correct in charging him with dangerous driving as opposed to careless driving (for which penalties are considerably less)?

If guilty, do you think Martin should be sent to prison and banned from driving?
- Speed limits are set to keep people safe and Martin broke the rules because he wanted to get his daughter's passport to the airport so she did not have to miss her flight to New Zealand.
- He may have had a reason for driving over the speed limit but it is at best an excuse.
- A fire engine trying to put out a blaze or an ambulance trying to get a seriously ill person to hospital would have had better reasons for exceeding speed limits.
- In the Crown Court, the *maximum* penalty for dangerous driving is two years' imprisonment, an unlimited fine, but penalties can be less.
- Dangerous driving does, however, carry a *minimum* obligatory driving ban of one year – before a driving licence can be reinstated, Martin will have to take an extended driving test if found guilty of dangerous driving.
- One of the factors to decide whether Martin was sent to prison is whether this is a first offence or whether he has other motoring convictions.

If Martin is found guilty, what reasons for a lenient sentence could his lawyers offer before he is sentenced?
- The most severe sentences for those found guilty of dangerous driving tend to be reserved for cases where alcohol or drugs contribute to the dangerous driving, where speed is grossly excessive, where drivers were racing against each other and where significant injury or damage is sustained.
- Martin's lawyers could explain why he was driving above the speed limit but point out there was no element of drugs or alcohol or racing in his behaviour – if he was a person of good character and this was his first conviction, they would certainly emphasise that point.
- However, the court would note that Martin was driving at a speed 50% above the limit and that some injury was sustained by the elderly woman – the more serious her injuries, the greater the chance Martin will go to prison.

Margin questions

Anyone over the age of 18 can be a juror. How would you feel if you were asked to be on a jury?
- The students could role play this issue.
- All jurors are supposed to hear the evidence and reach a conclusion over whether the accused is innocent or guilty.
- However, if a juror empathises with either the victim or the accused, this may influence the decision they reach.
- Sometimes jurors may have very stereotypical views about people from whichever group the accused seems to come. Would a Jewish juror feel able to judge fairly the acts of an accused Muslim – or vice versa?

CITIZENSHIP STUDIES

- How might a woman who desperately wanted a baby regard a mother accused of murdering her baby?
- If a juror who used recreational drugs was asked to decide whether another drug user was guilty, might he/she find the person 'not guilty' as a matter of principle?

Review and research

Should magistrates and judges be from a wider cross-section of society?
Originally magistrates were authority figures such as owners of businesses, local squires or other members of the aristocracy – and almost exclusively male. Big efforts have been made in recent years to ensure magistrates represent a fair cross-section of society – more women with fair representation of young and old, as well as people from ethnic minorities. The same efforts have been made in the appointment of judges. Being a magistrate or judge calls for an ability to apply complex rules and, as education levels improve, it is more feasible for a wider cross-section of society to be represented. A criticism of some magistrates is that they allow the professionally-qualified Clerk of the Court to exert too much influence over the decisions (innocence, guilt, sentencing) they reach.

Do we need to divide the legal profession between solicitors and barristers?
- Many of the roles filled by barristers (such as appearing in higher courts) can now be undertaken by solicitors.
- Most barristers specialise in particular areas of law and become authorities in that area (e.g. family law, company law, property law) and often go on to become judges.
- Most solicitors deal directly with members of the general public while barristers are approached only via solicitors.
- Many solicitors appear in lower courts rarely or not at all, concentrating instead on conveyancing property, writing wills or organising divorce petitions.
- Even if all barristers and solicitors were merged into a general category of 'lawyers' it is inevitable that the specialisations that exist at present would continue and in practice very little difference might be noticed.

Should juries continue in UK courts?
- Although an individual juror may want to believe a particular accused is innocent or guilty, the strength of the jury system is that all twelve (or at least ten) jurors need to agree for a verdict to be accepted.
- The right of an accused person for his or her case to be judged by fellow human beings from the same community is an important one.
- When a trial is complicated and takes a long time, the role of juror may be difficult for someone with family responsibilities or of limited education – such cases have sometimes collapsed because jurors found it impossible to make up their minds or agree.
- The jury system in the UK goes back centuries – is there really any reason to change it?

Crime and punishment

Lesson objectives	Specification link: Unit 1, Theme 2

By the end of this spread the student should:

• understand the role of prisons and the social characteristics of the prison population

• recognise the ways in which the justice system deals with crime and antisocial behaviour

Focus

...on whether prisons 'work' and the reasons for recidivism; look at the table comparing the social characteristics of the prison and general populations to consider whether other ways of dealing with crime might be more appropriate, including ASBOs, community punishments and restorative justice.

Key terms

• Anti-Social Behaviour Orders (ASBOs)

• community punishments

• deterrents

• Grendon Prison

• numeracy

• recidivism

• restorative justice

Linked activity sheets

• Crime

• The difference between civil and criminal law

Starter	Focus on the table. Ask the students how each element might explain the offenders' behaviour and whether alternative approaches might be appropriate in some cases.
Development	The first three characteristics show that those with an unsatisfactory life as a child are considerably more likely to be in prison than the population generally.
	The next six characteristics relate to school – those with fewest qualifications and reading/writing/number skills are much more likely to be in prison than the rest of the population.
	The final four criteria – mental disorders, drug use, hazardous drinking and unemployment – all see prisoners far more prominently represented than the general population.
	We don't know if more qualifications, reading/number skills, etc. and employment might enable someone to stay out of prison – in many prisons training is not given a high priority so prisoners are likely to be released with few if any more skills than when they arrived.
	Ask students to think why Grendon might make such a difference.
	Recidivism rates (being sent back to prison) are highest among younger prisoners with short sentences – older prisoners with longer sentences are less likely to reoffend.
	Focus on students' views on ASBOs, community punishments and restorative justice.
	The Howard League makes the interesting point that, if more people were treated in the community, reducing the prison population,

CITIZENSHIP STUDIES

	more attention could be given to the needs of those who do have to be locked up.
Plenary	Go over the *Checklist* points. Students could work on the *Further issues* questions as research or homework. Or you may want them to think about how better education, caring and job-finding services might be the best way to bring down crime figures further and faster.

Answers to questions in the Student Book

What's the issue?

How do prisoners differ from the rest of the population?
- Generally it seems that the upbringing of prisoners usually had more problems than that of most of the adult population (e.g. truanting, running away, being put into care, special needs, etc.).
- Consequently many prisoners have few if any qualifications and only a limited ability to read, write or deal with numbers.
- Prisoners are much more likely than the rest of the population to suffer from mental disorders and to have major problems with drug misuse and hazardous drinking.
- Given these circumstances, it is not surprising that prisoners are thirteen times more likely to be unemployed than the rest of the population.

How can you explain these differences?
- For some offenders, crime may offer the answer to a problem where there appears to be no other way out.
- If they had been better socialised, with a coherent set of moral values, they may have tried harder to avoid crime.
- In many cases, the problems seem to have started with family breakdown during childhood years.
- To overcome such problems government has emphasised the importance of eliminating social exclusion, involving greater emphasis on more children gaining qualifications and reading/writing/number skills so they can approach the world of work with greater self-confidence and chances of success.

Do the differences suggest there are more effective ways of treating offenders?
- Many prisoners leave prison stigmatised, without a family, and with broken home and employment connections – problems that are less likely to occur if people are punished in the community.
- Someone who starts to gain skills and perhaps qualifications after many years of having been without them is likely to gain self-esteem, be more confident and better able to take on and retain a job.
- For individuals who have run away from home, been taken into care, truanted from school and finished up with few reading, writing or number skills or qualifications, plus a drinking or drug problem, their lives aren't going to be turned round quickly or easily, especially if they now have mental health problems.
- Government claims to be 'tough on crime, tough on the causes of crime' have seen crime levels fall substantially but much progress still needs to be made in tackling the roots of crime – building more prisons may not be as good an idea as providing more mental health services or training for jobs.

Margin questions

Could alternative ways of dealing with offenders reduce the size of the prison population?
- Trying to tackle health problems and lack of skills instead of imprisoning offenders is an approach used in many EU countries. Estonia, Latvia, Lithuania and Poland send a substantially higher proportion of the population to prison than do England and Wales. However, *Social Trends 39* (can be downloaded free from the ONS website) has a diagram (Fig 9.16) showing that 20 of the 27 EU countries have a lower proportion of the population in prison than England and Wales.
- In answering this question refer to ASBOs, community punishments and the idea of restorative justice as further alternatives to prison.

Review and research

How can offending behaviour be explained?
If a person is brought up by parents to behave honestly and to have a secure set of moral values, showing a proper concern for others, such values will be enhanced in school and as they grow up into well grounded adults. Those without such an upbringing may lack the moral compass to know that offending should be avoided not because it can lead to punishment but because it is hurtful to others and therefore wrong.

Are deterrents successful or unsuccessful?
- Deterrents work only if detection is certain. Once detection is only a 'maybe', human nature will dictate that many people come to believe they can get away with committing an offence.
- Since only 27% of offences result in the offender's being identified, the scope for not being caught is high and therefore any deterrent effect may be weak.
- Undoubtedly deterrents do have some effect – but the death penalty in the USA and China and canings in Singapore and Malaysia do not stop some people continuing to commit crimes that can attract such punishments in those countries.

What are the best ways to tackle offending behaviour?
- Debate this in class. Probably different responses are appropriate for different offending behaviour.
- Students often become unbelievably harsh when asked such questions.
- Don't let them forget that human rights apply to offenders as much as victims.

What are the advantages and disadvantages of replacing many prison sentences with community punishments?
- Making people who have offended work in the community. This can help the community and also give the offender a sense of making good the harm done by the offence.
- Some people given community punishments do reoffend but generally fewer than those sent to prison.
- Organising community work and drug or alcohol rehabilitation or adult training programmes in the community is generally more effective and less costly than trying to do such things in prison.
- Some offenders are too dangerous to allow to be free – some will need to be held in secure units until mental health problems have been overcome and society needs to be protected from others who are sane but dangerous. That is the justification for long periods of imprisonment (including whole of life imprisonment in the case of the most dangerous criminals).

CITIZENSHIP STUDIES

Getting a decision: the purpose of civil law

Lesson objectives	Specification link: Unit 1, Theme 2
By the end of this spread the student should: • understand how civil law differs from criminal law • recognise the wide range of civil cases • understand which courts deal with civil cases	

Focus

...on the difference between criminal cases (leading to punishment of the guilty) and civil cases (leading to a decision to resolve a dispute – e.g. over a contract, custody of a child, divorce, dismissal from a job or a will).

Key terms

• arbitration

• bankruptcy

• claimant

• compensation

• contract

• custody of a child

• defamation, libel and slander

• divorce

• legal aid

• mediation

• tribunals

• wrongful dismissal

Linked activity sheets

• Heart transplant

• The difference between civil and criminal law

Starter	How is a fine for speeding (crime) different from being ordered to pay compensation for an accident (civil case)? In the crime the individual is punished and the cash goes to the state; in the civil case the compensation goes to the claimant who has suffered wrong.
Development	Use the examples in *What's the issue?* to highlight the differences between civil and criminal law and the outcomes of both kinds of case. Then link cases to courts – discuss which cases are dealt with where. Make sure students are familiar with key terms and can use them confidently. Leave plenty of time to discuss why cases are so expensive (involving the time of specialist barristers, solicitors, a judge and other highly qualified/paid staff). What would be the advantages and disadvantages of taking a case to the Small Claims Court? If cases are so expensive, does this mean unfairness for those who are denied legal aid? (See http://www.legalservices.gov.uk/ website.) Would better decisions be reached in civil cases if decisions were

CITIZENSHIP STUDIES

	reached informally through counselling, mediation or arbitration services?
Plenary	Go over the *Checklist* points. Students could work on the *Further issues* questions as research or homework. Or you may want them to find out about the nearest court dealing with civil cases and how claims are resolved.

Answers to questions in the Student Book

What's the issue?

Why do most criminal cases result in the accused going to court?
- Most cases involving a crime go to court so the court can decide if an individual is innocent or guilty.
- If found guilty, the accused's lawyers offer reasons (mitigation) why a lighter sentence should be given.
- The magistrates or judge will then announce the punishment the offender will receive.

Are courts the best way to deal with civil cases?
- Court hearings can be very confrontational and bringing expensive teams of lawyers together can take quite a long time and be very costly.
- To avoid this, attempts have been made to find cheaper and non-confrontational ways to resolve a dispute.

What other methods could be used to decide cases?
- Increasingly in recent years people have turned to counselling, mediation and arbitration services, which try to find solutions to disputes on which everyone concerned can agree.
- Such solutions may subsequently be endorsed by a judge.

Margin questions

How does a fine in a criminal court differ from compensation ordered in a civil court?
A fine imposed by a criminal court goes to local or national government whereas compensation (e.g. for injury) goes to the individual who has been injured.

Review and research

Could more cases be dealt with informally rather than going to court?
Many motoring and some other offences are now dealt with by fixed penalty fines so it is no longer necessary for an accused to go to court, unless denying guilt. Sometimes drivers involved in motor accidents are offered the chance to go on Driver Improvement Programmes rather than face prosecution. Those who commit other less serious offences may be cautioned rather than being taken to court and punished. In civil cases there is already an increasing trend towards people turning to counselling, mediation and arbitration services rather than taking a dispute to court.

Do legal aid rules mean some people are denied access to justice?
The Legal Services Commission runs the legal aid scheme in England and Wales. The Community Legal Service helps people with civil legal problems such as family breakdown, debt and housing while the Criminal Defence Service helps people who are under police investigation or facing criminal charges. In recent years the support available for civil litigants or for those accused of criminal offences has been severely restricted. Although the *very* poor are supported, many others are not. Some campaigners believe that legal aid should be as available as treatment on the NHS when we are ill. Otherwise, they say, justice will be available to those with a lot of money who can afford to buy it, not to the rest.

Why are court hearings so expensive: could costs be reduced?

- A skilled lawyer may be able to charge up to £10,000 per day for her or his services and even less eminent lawyers may charge £200 or £500 per day – to cover time spent working on a case as well as time appearing in court.
- A case outside London involving one more and one less expensive lawyer on each side and lasting ten days, having taken ten days to complete preliminary work and interview witnesses prior to the court hearing, could easily cost in the region of £50,000.
- In reality there are many other costs in criminal cases – paying the expenses of the jury, paying a salary to the judge and other court officials, as well as the background work that goes into deciding whether a case will be brought in the first place.
- Most criminal cases are decided in magistrates' courts where, usually, cases are argued by solicitors rather than barristers and where there is no jury.
- It would be a mistake to look for reforms just to cut costs – criminal courts deal with people's reputations and (where a prison sentence is a possibility) their freedom – so it is important that decisions are taken carefully and impartially by highly skilled minds.
- Fast-track approaches such as deciding modest civil claims in a Small Claims Court, can greatly reduce the time involved and no court costs are awarded for cases up to about £10,000 in value – though a litigant will have to meet any costs she or he incurs.
- Counselling, arbitration and mediation procedures are much cheaper than going for a full court hearing in civil cases.

Settling disputes

Lesson objectives	Specification link: Unit 1, Theme 2
By the end of this spread the student should: • have a good understanding of civil law relating to employment, consumer rights and the family	

Focus

...on four areas of civil disputes – employment, consumer rights, the family and wills – this is not to say that other matters such as bankruptcy or defamation are not important but the main focus of the Citizenship course is the four items highlighted.

Key terms

- consumer
- contract
- custody (e.g. residency and contact orders)
- Citizens Advice Bureau
- dismissal

- employment tribunal
- gross misconduct
- redundancy
- verbal, written and final warnings
- wills (and deeds of variation)

Linked activity sheets

- The difference between civil and criminal law

Starter	Begin with contracts – what are they? When we buy a ticket on a bus or to go to the cinema we enter into a contract. If we have a part-time job and receive a wage, that involves a contract. Marriage is a contract and, when disputes arise over such contracts, the civil law exists to deal with them.
Development	If students have a part-time job, get them to think about their own and the employer's rights and responsibilities. What happens if either side breaks the rules? See *Employment rights*. Then ask them to think about their rights and responsibilities if they go to buy some jeans. When are they entitled to their money back? When is a shop right to refuse to return money or offer to exchange goods instead? Marriages increasingly break down – don't lose sight of the ethical as well as the legal aspect in discussing this. The welfare of children from broken homes needs to be discussed in terms of the four different types of orders that courts may use. Why might arbitration, counselling and mediation services prove a better solution than going to court? Finally discuss inheritance, intestacy, wills and why deeds of variation may be needed. Why might someone not make a will? What circumstances may make someone's will become out of date?

Plenary	Go over the *Checklist* points. Students could work on the *Further issues* questions as research or homework. Or you may want them to think about similarities and differences between the many very different contracts discussed: employment, buying and selling, marriage.

Answers to questions in the Student Book

What's the issue?

What legal rights do consumers and employees have?

- Many of the rights enjoyed by consumers are listed on p. 26. Although people expect to sign a document when they arrange a loan at the bank or buy goods through a hire purchase agreement, many contracts into which we enter as consumers are not written down as such – there is a contractual relationship when we buy a ticket to travel on a train or bus or go the cinema or a football match.
- Employer and employee rights are discussed on pp. 28-29 and p. 52. The most important source of such rights is the contract of employment, which may to some extent vary from firm to firm; however contracts of employment cannot be at odds with the law of the land and all laws apply regardless of what a contract of employment says.

Why is it always important to read all the 'small print' in a contract before signing it?

- The 'small print' is where the detailed rules in an agreement are set down.
- For example, deep in the small print some credit card companies say that, if a monthly payment arrives after a specified date, any concessionary rate for the first year of the card's life will be cancelled immediately.
- This means that the interest rate charged on an outstanding balance could rise from 5% to 25% just because the consumer had not been fully aware of the rules.

If you have a dispute, how could the Citizens Advice Bureau (CAB) help you sort it out?

- There are CAB offices throughout the UK, mainly staffed by skilled volunteers.
- If you need to know which organisation deals with unsafe food, unreasonable credit agreements, unfair employment practices or income tax problems, they will be able to put you in touch with people who can help and advise you or websites where information you need may be found.
- CABs are friendly, well informed and impartial and can help everyone to find out about their rights.

Margin questions

How do employees know if they are working safely and have been trained properly?

All employees are protected by the Health and Safety at Work laws. Good employers will recognise the importance of their staff working safely and provide training and suitable safety equipment. If workers feel they are being asked to operate in unsafe conditions, such matters are customarily raised by trade union or safety representatives.

How and why are dismissal and redundancy treated differently?

Dismissal means that someone's contract of employment is ended because of unsatisfactory conduct or performance; the employer is likely to replace the person as quickly as possible because there is still a need to employ such a post-holder. Redundancy means that a firm no longer needs or can no longer afford to employ someone in a particular post, so once the employee has left the firm the post will not be filled by another worker. A dismissed worker will generally be paid wages due and may be given a period of notice to work out during which a normal wage will be paid. Workers made redundant generally receive a compensation payment set down on a scale by the firm, which is usually more generous than the government or 'statutory scheme' of:

- 0.5 weeks' pay for each full year of service where age during year less than 22
- weeks' pay for each full year of service where age during year is 22 or above, but less than 41
- 1.5 weeks' pay for each full year of service where age during year is 41+.

Review and research

How can people ensure they are aware of their rights?

Rights don't mean much until they are incorporated into the laws. Subjects like Citizenship Studies ensure many more young people now have a greater awareness of their rights. Where a particular query arises, the local Citizens Advice Bureau or appropriate websites are probably the most reliable sources of good information.

Why do many workers not join trade unions?

- In the days when workers often expected to work for the same firm for all or most of their working lives, it was natural to be a member of a trade union. Sometimes it is obligatory to join the union.
- As more people become more qualified, they often feel able to switch jobs, move from one employer to another, take career breaks and/or accept a series of short-term contracts.
- In such a situation trade union membership is less appropriate.
- However, when the economic climate is uncertain and there is a possibility of substantial numbers of workers being made redundant, many people view union membership as an important protection for their rights.

Why do some employers not want their employees to join trade unions?

- Good employers welcome the existence of trade unions so they can have coherent discussions over any matters of concern with trade union representatives.
- Less enlightened employers may not want a trade union to be keeping an eye on them, ready to point out any breaches in employment law or acknowledged good practice.
- Trade unions may take up the case of individual workers who may have been treated unfairly, may negotiate for improvements in pay or working conditions and they will expect to see changes in employment law being implemented in places of employment where they have members.

Does the law protect children enough?

- Cases that have attracted newspaper headlines, such as those of Victoria Climbié and Baby Peter in Haringey, suggest not.
- There are, however, clear guidelines on the orders courts may issue if parents cannot agree arrangements for their children when their relationship breaks up (see p53).
- An important part of the protection children need (especially if their parents are separated) is adequate financial support. In the past the Child Support Agency (CSA) was strongly criticised for leaving so many children and single parents in poverty, though the organisation claimed in 2009 that its performance was now much stronger.

CITIZENSHIP STUDIES

Democracy at work: The people speak

Lesson objectives	Specification link: Unit 1, Theme 2
By the end of this spread the student should: • understand the main elements of parliamentary democracy and patterns of voting in elections and referendums • recognise alternative forms of participation • understand the importance of empathy in helping to develop our opinions	

Focus

...on representative democracy (voting for representatives such as councillors or MPs) and direct democracy (directly deciding in referendums); also consider the importance of party records in office and promises for the future in helping to explain voting behaviour.

Key terms

• democracy

• general election

• majority vote

• middle class and working class

• political parties

• pressure groups

• referendum

• voting turnout

Linked activity sheets

• Democracy in action

• The structure of government

Starter	Start off with X Factor voting – ask students to focus on the differences between voting in a general (or local) election and voting in reality TV shows.
Development	Then focus on whether voting choices are based on a party's past performance (record in office locally or nationally) or their future promises.
	Is it right that the working class = Labour/ middle class = Conservative belief is less true nowadays, not least because people's class identifications are weakening?
	Although much publicity during a general election campaign is about who will form the next government (Labour v Conservative for the last 60 years+), in many constituencies a third party (Nationalists or Liberal Democrats) is the main choice against either Labour or Conservative but not both.
	Will Citizenship Studies give young people more confidence to go and vote – especially when there are issues about which they feel strongly (as university students in university towns did in 2005)?
	Are people well enough informed to take the final decisions in referendums (Europe, Scottish and Welsh devolution, Good Friday Agreement, Regional Assemblies in England, elected mayors) – does it matter if they make decisions on gut feelings?

CITIZENSHIP STUDIES

	Often voters express feelings through the pressure groups they join; the groups then campaign for the outcomes their members favour.
Plenary	Go over the *Checklist* points. Students may work on the *Further issues* questions as research or homework. Or you may want them to look at their local council website to find out the most recent election results at council or parliamentary or European level in the area.

Answers to questions in the Student Book

What's the issue?

What difference would it make if people could vote as many times as they liked in UK general elections?
- The rule is that each person should vote just once. This is the big difference between real elections and television events such as *X Factor* or *Strictly Come Dancing* where supporters of particular artists could vote as many times as they wished.

What problems could arise if people just voted based on the personality of political candidates rather than policies or their previous record in office?
- If people voted on personality rather than policy, they might find they had elected someone to represent them who believed in many things they opposed – someone on a low wage might find they had elected someone who believed everyone (rich or poor) should pay a flat rate tax so a rich person would pay no more than a poor person (obviously unjust).
- Or someone who favoured 'green' policies might find they had elected someone who operated oil wells and claimed (in spite of all the evidence) that there was no such thing as global warming and no need to restrict the use of fossil fuels or to worry about the prospect of climate change.
- Alternatively, someone might offer a set of sensible-sounding policies but their past record in office might have been far from successful.

Why is it important for people to be able to keep their vote secret if they want to?
- Everyone has the right to privacy, so individuals who want to keep the way they vote a secret have a right to do so.
- In some families, different family members vote for different parties, so some of the family may feel that not saying how they voted is a good way not to offend anyone.
- There have been suggestions in the past that sometimes employers and manufacturers preferred to employ and do deals with people on the same side as themselves. In the nineteenth century, people were sometimes evicted from their homes if the landlord thought they had voted for a party different from the one he supported.
- Such behaviour would be intolerable if it occurred today, yet some people prefer to keep their affairs private, just in case.

Margin questions

Why might Labour MPs sometimes not support a Labour government or why might Conservative or Liberal Democrat MPs sometimes go against the official views of their party?
- Sometimes particular circumstances in an MP's constituency may lead the MP to believe a different policy would be more appropriate.
- On some issues (especially if the party made no promises about the topic in its manifesto prior to the election), an MP may disagree with the line the party leadership decides to take – e.g. Labour and whether former Gurkha soldiers should be allowed to settle in the UK.
- Sometimes MPs from the same party may take different attitudes towards a new issue that arises, e.g. how to react to the tyrannical government of Robert Mugabe in Zimbabwe or to the Chinese government's suppression of human rights in Tibet.
- On some conscience issues such as abortion, use of human embryos, and assisted suicide, some MPs may feel so strongly that, even if their party adopted an 'official line', they might not feel able to support it.

CITIZENSHIP STUDIES

What are the advantages and disadvantages of giving a bigger say to the general public in referendums?

Advantages
- Referendums can help to reconnect voters with politics and democracy, reducing apathy and abstention.
- They can help to resolve political problems, where a governing party is divided over an issue, as Labour was over Europe in 1975.
- If a government wants specific approval for a change to the constitution, a referendum provides a way of doing this – referendums were used to decide whether elected mayors should be appointed and whether central government powers should be devolved to Scotland, Wales, Northern Ireland and the north-east of England.
- If voters could call for a vote on whether a specific government policy should go ahead, this would mean governments would listen more closely to public opinion and not lose touch.

Disadvantages
- Referendums undermine the role and importance of elected representatives such as MPs and councillors by taking some decisions out of their hands.
- It is sometimes questioned whether voters have the knowledge and understanding to make informed decisions about complicated issues such as the state of the economy.
- Opponents of referendums also argue that, if the executive has the power to decide when referendums are held, they can be used as a political tool to suit the needs of the governing party rather than the interests of democracy.
- Turnout at referendums is often lower than at national elections so it cannot be claimed that referendums increase the legitimacy or authority of political decisions.

Review and research

How could voting be made easier and more popular?
See the Electoral Commission website. It has conducted trials and experiments with postal voting, voting by text and voting using the Internet. It has also been suggested that elections might be held at weekends when more people have time off from work rather than in the middle of the working week – on Thursdays – as at present.

Are young voters given enough information to decide how to vote?
- At present debate continues over whether young people aged 16 should be allowed to vote, since they can marry and join the armed forces at that age.
- One argument in favour is that, if young people have studied Citizenship, they are much more likely to be aware of political issues than previous generations of young people.
- The 2005 general election demonstrated (e.g. in university towns) that turnouts among young voters rose when they were faced with issues about which they felt strongly.

How can other forms of participation change things?
- Someone who feels strongly in favour of a project can undertake voluntary work to support it.
- They can engage in fund-raising activities to support causes they favour.
- People may join pressure groups that promote policies they support and take part in events, demonstrations, etc.
- They can share their ideas by writing to newspapers or producing a regular blog or submitting feedback to newspaper blogs on particular stories or to the websites of radio and television stations.
- One of the most direct ways in which people can make a difference is to contribute to government or local government consultations and give reasons why they do or do not favour a particular proposal.

Elections

Lesson objectives	Specification link: Unit 1, Theme 2

By the end of this spread the student should:

• understand that elections are held in the UK for councils, devolved bodies (Scotland, Wales, Northern Ireland), Parliament and the European Parliament

• know the arguments for and against the 'first-past-the-post' and other systems of voting in the UK

• recognise reasons why some people may choose not to vote in elections

Focus

...on the strengths and weaknesses of the first-past-the-post and other voting systems, knowing which systems operate for which elections. Emphasise that for all elections except the Westminster Parliament members serve for a fixed number of years.

Key terms

• Additional Member System

• first-past-the-post system

• fixed terms

• proportional representation (PR)

• Regional List system

• Single Transferable Vote System

• turnout

• winner's bonus

Linked activity sheets

• The great biscuit election

• Democracy in action

• The structure of government

Starter	Start off with the 'problem'. Explain how the mismatch between seats and votes and the 'winner's bonus' come about.
Development	To take an example, in the six constituencies in Cumbria in 2005, Labour won 4 seats, Con 1 and Lib Dems 1 but when all the votes had been added together the Con had 38.2% of votes, Labour 34.6% and the Lib Dems 23.3%. If the whole area had been one constituency with six MPs, a PR system would probably have resulted in Con 3 (+2), Labour 2 (-2), Lib Dem 1 (=).
	Distortion is also evident in London – Labour won 1.12m votes (44 MPs), Con 0.92 m (21 MPs), Lib Dems 0.63m (8 MPs) whereas a 'fair shares' split (where the shares of seats and votes gained were the same) would have been approx Labour 31 (-13), Con 25 (+4), Lib Dems 17 (+9).
	Those who favour the present system see its strength being that one party has an overall majority (e.g. Labour 2005). That leads to decisive government, though critics might say not always popular or effective government.
	The alternative would be a coalition government (as in the Welsh and Northern Irish devolved bodies) or a minority government (as in the Scottish devolved body in 2009).

	Advocates for electoral reform say that, while one party would always prefer to be in charge, coalition or minority governments can be made to work perfectly effectively. Details of different voting systems are briefly outlined in the glossary.
	Non-voting in elections is a serious problem since most people want their rights but therefore need to act responsibly and take part in elections – debate this with the students.
Plenary	Go over the *Checklist* points. Students could work on the *Further issues* questions as research or homework. Or you may want them to research the differences between the various PR systems. (See Electorial Reform Society website.)

Answers to questions in the Student Book

What's the issue?

Why are the shares of seats in Parliament so different from the shares of votes? Does it matter?

- Imagine there are 100 MPs to be elected and 1,000 people vote in each single member constituency using first past the post.
- If one party were to win every seat except one by a majority of 4 and the second party won just one seat by a margin of 400 votes, the second party with one seat would have four more votes overall than the other party with 99 seats.
- This is how distorted results can occur with first past the post, as in the Cumbria example.
- With 100 'mini contests' in the example above there is no guarantee that the share of votes would have any similarity to the share of seats.

If the first-past-the-post system gives winners a big bonus of seats, why would they want to change the system?

- Even the beneficiaries of the present system sometimes find the system difficult or even embarrassing to defend.
- It is noticeable that the new bodies set up in recent years - European Parliament, Northern Ireland Assembly, Welsh Assembly, Scottish Parliament and Greater London Assembly - all use a form of proportional representation.
- In Scotland, local government councils are now elected by single transferable vote - a form of PR.
- The most likely reason Labour or Conservatives might give their support to a proportional representation system being used for elections to Westminster would be if this became a condition advanced by Liberal Democrats for gaining support for a minority or coalition government in a hung Parliament situation in which no one party had a majority over all others.

Margin questions

Would you be more likely to go and vote if someone came to see you and spoke to you rather than sending leaflets, texting or telephoning?

- In the 1950s when turnouts in general elections sometimes exceeded 80%, television was in its infancy, political reporting on the radio was very limited and most people received calls at home from the different political parties, all trying to get the voter to support their candidate.
- On election day each party had lists of thousands of voters they expected would support them and the job was to get a higher share of 'their' people to vote than other parties.
- This often meant that voters were more aware of different candidates than nowadays because often they had met them personally or attended political meetings where a candidate would speak.
- Today we experience 24-hour news on television and, instead of canvassing, political parties try to win our support through leaflets, telephoning and texting.
- There is much less personal contact now than in the 1950s and it is sometimes suggested this change has led to the fall in turnout, which was around 60% in the 2001 and 2005 general elections.

Review and research

Are the benefits of changing the system greater than the disadvantages?

The main reason often advanced for retaining the first-past-the-post system is that it provides stable, one-party government. Yet stable, one-party government has been much criticised as being ineffective. Evidence from the devolved bodies suggests that coalition and minority governments can be made to work perfectly satisfactorily (as such bodies do in many EU countries) so perhaps the disadvantage of PR is not as great as its opponents suggest!

Would a ruling party that benefits from the present system ever be likely to change it?

As suggested above, the adoption of a new voting system might be the condition a third party such as the Liberal Democrats might impose in return for their participation in a coalition or minority government in a hung Parliament where no one party had an overall majority.

How can more people be encouraged to participate?

- Generally, election turnouts are highest when the result is tightly contested. Writing this in May 2009, it may be that the intensity of the contest at the next General Election will see many more people taking an interest and voting than in the last few elections.
- Although the membership of the Labour and Conservative parties has sharply declined, the past 20 years have seen substantial advances by other parties such as Greens, UKIP, Liberal Democrats, Democratic Unionist and Sinn Fein.
- Overall memberships of political parties may be down, but memberships of pressure groups have increased sharply (see p68).
- Many more people today give feedback to newspapers (letters to the editor and responses to news stories via the Internet) and to radio and television stations.
- Government now tends to be much more open and some consultation exercises attract large volumes of comments and suggestions.

CITIZENSHIP STUDIES

Political parties

Lesson objectives	Specification link: Unit 1, Theme 2
By the end of this spread the student should: • know about political parties in and out of Parliament • recognise the policy differences and success rates of the main political parties • understand the ways in which political parties try to win support	

Focus

...on the main differences between parties, their core beliefs and the significance of the leaders of the three main parties; students should recognise that some parties are genuinely national, some regional, some local, some exist at all these levels and others just exist for 'fun'.

Key terms

• ballot paper

• coalition and minority government

• Conservative, Labour and Liberal Democrat parties

• Electoral Commission

• focus groups and opinion polls

• public and private sectors

• social exclusion

• Welfare State

Linked activity sheets

• The structure of government

Starter	Start with a council or parliamentary election result in your area (from a local council or newspaper website). Students should brainstorm why people vote as they do.
Development	There will probably be candidates from the main parties as well as candidates from parties with no MPs but which have members in Europe, the devolved bodies or the Greater London Assembly – UKIP, Greens.
	In the past Labour's main support was from the working class, Conservatives from middle class and Lib Dems most evenly across the classes. Class and party identifications now seem to be much weaker, causing bigger swings at elections.
	For policy differences focus on the *Different party, different policy* section on page 73.
	Often voting is influenced by local traditions – Lib Dems and Labour had greatest support historically in areas where nonconformist religious beliefs were strong (hence Lib Dem strength in Cornwall); it used to be said that the Church of England was the 'Conservative Party at prayer'.
	What other local traditions might influence election results?
	Personalities can be important – party leaders or individual MPs or candidates; a long-standing MP may build up a substantial 'personal vote' in an area.

	In 2008 'fun' candidates stood in three by-elections (e.g. David Bishop gained 44 votes in Haltemprice as candidate for the Church of the Militant Elvis Party). Although the support was modest, it was a way for voters to demonstrate their disapproval of the main parties and their policies.
Plenary	Go over the *Checklist* points. Students could work on the *Further issues* questions as research or homework. Or you may want them to research policy differences on the websites of the main parties.

Answers to questions in the Student Book

What's the issue?

Why do you think people shift their support from one party to another?

- *They haven't delivered* - When Tony Blair and Labour defeated John Major and the Conservatives in 1997, Labour campaigned on the theme 'things can only get better'. People who do not believe things have got better may feel some disappointment and change the party they vote for.
- *New Issue* - Sometimes voters attach great importance to one issue – voters who favour green policies may switch support to another party that appears more committed to the goals they now favour.
- *Policy for the future* - If one party changes its policy on an issue (e.g. inheritance tax), people who could benefit from the new policy may support the party whose new policy they favour.
- *Tactical voting* – If voters think one party has a better chance of defeating a party they dislike, they may switch their support away from the party they like best.
- *Glasgow East by-election* – In the 2008 by-election, Labour support dropped from 60.7% to 41.7% (record), while the SNP vote rose from 17% to 43.1% (policy for the future) but the SNP might not have won if they had not also squeezed the votes of the Liberal Democrats from 11.8% to 3.5% (tactical) and also reduced the Conservative share of the vote.

When or why might people vote for a mainly local party?

- If a local party suddenly forms and gains support to promote a local issue, it may attract substantial support in the short term at least.
- A good example was in Wyre Forest, where there were threats to close Kidderminster Hospital.
- Opponents of this took control of the local council and, in 2001, local hospital consultant Dr Richard Taylor was elected as Health Concern MP, gaining 58% of the vote and a majority of 17,630.
- By 2005, when Dr Taylor was re-elected, his vote was down to 40%, with a reduced majority of 5,250.
- In neither election was Dr Taylor opposed by Liberal Democrats, who had run the council in the 1970s and 1980s.
- Once a range of services at Kidderminster Hospital had been retained, the issue became less compelling for local voters and by 2009 Health Concern held just 10 of the 42 seats on the council.

Why might someone decide to support a 'fun' party, for example, the Fancy Dress Party?

- Voting for a 'fun' party means doing your duty by voting but shows you do not support other political parties.
- The higher the support gained by 'fun' candidates, the clearer the dissatisfaction with established parties becomes.
- Sometimes joke candidates do get elected, as Alan Hope did, becoming a member of Ashburton Town Council in Devon, representing the Official Monster Raving Loony Party.

Margin questions

All the MPs in Cornwall are Liberal Democrats, in Surrey they are Conservatives and in Tyne and Wear they are Labour. Why are some national parties more successful in some areas than others?

As indicated above, key factors will be:
- strength of a party's organisation and campaigning
- how well its policies match the demographic balance of the local population (e.g. Conservative Party unlikely to be successful in area with large numbers of unskilled working class or unemployed voters),

- local traditions including religious leanings.

In most areas there are usually two main parties who fight for power, with other parties having little chance of success. In London the main contenders for power are Labour and Conservative with Ken Livingstone (Labour) having been mayor until he was replaced by Boris Johnson (Conservative) but in many areas it is now less likely that the two parties will be Labour and Conservative. In north-west Wales it is Plaid Cymru and Labour; in urban cities such as Hull, Sheffield, Leeds, Manchester, Liverpool and Newcastle-on-Tyne the contest is between Labour and Liberal Democrats while in Devon, Dorset, Cornwall and Somerset the battle is usually between Conservatives and Liberal Democrats.

Review and research

Why has the number of political parties increased in recent years but party memberships fallen?

In 1951 most constituencies in the general election had just Labour and Conservative candidates. Both parties contained many people who agreed in general but who also had many different points of view or priorities. Since the 1980s people have been less ready to identify with a party with which they disagree on some key parts of policy, leading to splits and breakaways. The Greens might in the past have been in the Labour or Liberal parties; UKIP members might previously have been Conservatives; Scottish and Welsh Nationalists might have previously been unhappy supporters of the other parties. In 1951 Leominster (Herefordshire) had just Labour and Conservative candidates. By 2005 there were five candidates – in order of support, Conservative, Liberal Democrat, Labour, Greens and UKIP. In recent years there has also been a decline in the numbers of people paying subscriptions to political parties – one reason for this is that many more people now give financial support to particular causes, so while party memberships have fallen, memberships of pressure groups have increased substantially.

Are UK parties democratic enough?

- Up to the 1970s rank-and-file party members had little influence over who was chosen as the leader of their party; the leaders of the Labour, Conservative and Liberal Democrat parties are now all elected by party members.
- Policies were confirmed at party conferences but many big decisions were taken behind the scenes with party members able to exercise less influence than they wished – they could put forward policies to party conferences but, even when passed, it wasn't guaranteed that the party leadership would promote them.
- Greater accountability now occurs in all parties with candidates being reselected (or not) prior to each election, giving some power to local parties.
- Most parties now try to 'manage' their party conferences to minimise the chance of appearing disunited or having policy rows that get out of hand – such management often leads to campaigns to make parties more democratic.

Why is the idea of state funding for political parties gaining support?

In a democracy all parties need to be able to put over their case effectively but if some parties have much greater resources than others, this can create unfairness. Both Labour and Conservatives have been heavily in debt in recent years. It is suggested by some that election expenditures should be drastically reduced and individual donations limited, with some financial support coming from taxpayers through the state.

Representation

Lesson objectives	Specification link: Unit 1, Theme 2
By the end of this spread the student should: • recognise the socio-economic profile of MPs • understand the relationship between constituents and MPs • know about the duties and functions of an MP – and how free an MP is to act as she or he pleases	

Focus

...on how much freedom MPs have from control by their parties, how socially diverse their backgrounds are, the roles they actually fulfil and the things they do in a typical week.

Key terms

• adjournment debate

• civil servants

• constituency

• councillors

• direct and representative democracy

• MPs' blogs and websites

• ombudsman

• private member's bill

• Question Time

• select committee

Linked activity sheets

• The structure of government

Starter	Start with your MP or councillor. How representative are they to the area they represent – age, sex, religion, colour, beliefs, where they live, the job they did before becoming an MP? Do such social factors matter?
Development	If MPs were all over 50, they might not understand the problems of young adults and families today. Even though women are still in a minority, the election of over 100 women MPs has ensured Parliament looks at family, children's and women's issues more sensitively. Ethnic minorities are still under-represented but they do now have some representation – a person from an ethnic minority doing the work of an MP promotes acceptance of people from minorities as people who contribute positively to society. The constituency with barely 20,000 voters is known by its Gaelic name as Na h-Eileanan an Iar; the constituency with over 100,000 voters is the Isle of Wight. This means one MP has five times more constituents to represent than the other - conducting surgeries to deal with problems, writing letters to or having meetings with ministers, maintaining close contact with local councils and other organisations, asking questions in Parliament and raising constituency concerns in an adjournment debate or private member's bill. Ensure students know the five types of activities MPs engage in: (i) representing constituents, speaking out on issues, (ii) debating,

	amending and voting on legislation (new laws), (iii) checking on government activities through questions, etc., (iv) serving in government, (v) authorising and reviewing taxation and government expenditure.
	Political parties pay most of the costs of electing an MP so they expect the MP to support the party line most of the time – but voters like MPs who act independently for conscience or policy reasons.
Plenary	Go over the *Checklist* points. Students could work on the *Further issues* questions as research or homework. Or you may want them to look at the websites of different MPs to get an idea of what they do and how much they involve constituents in their work.

Answers to questions in the Student Book

What's the issue?

Is 100,000 people too many for one MP to represent?
- The biggest constituency with over 100,000 voters is the Isle of Wight – a relatively compact area.
- So it is probably no more difficult for the MP to run advice surgeries in island's main towns than if the population was nearer the national average for a constituency of 70,000.
- The above average number of voters may mean that the MP has more personal problems to try to sort out, which may greatly increase his workload, needing to write more letters, have more meetings with ministers, ask more questions in Parliament, etc.
- A related issue is whether it is right in a democracy for votes to have different values. The winner on the Isle of Wight gained 32,717 votes but the second-placed candidate gained 19,739, which would have been more than enough votes to win in many other constituencies and even the third-placed candidate who secured 11,484 votes could have been elected with that number of votes in other areas.
- In the constituency with the smallest electorate, Na h-Eileanan an Iar, the MP was elected with just 6,213 votes – so while the UK operates a system of one person, one vote, it does not guarantee that all votes have equal value.

As they are elected as a member of a particular party, should MPs always vote as their party says? When might it be justifiable for an MP not to follow the party line?
- Most people vote for a political party because of its policies (stated in the party manifesto) and its leadership – especially if they like the leader and trust the team of senior spokespeople.
- Sometimes issues arise in a constituency where the party line may not suit the constituents or their MP – for example while the Labour government is in favour of constructing another runway for Heathrow Airport in West London, the local Labour MP campaigns hotly against this and reflects the wishes and concerns of his constituents in Hayes and Harlington in doing so.
- Conscience issues will also affect how an MP votes. Martin Salter, Labour MP for Reading West, believed the government was wrong to try to limit the numbers of Gurkha soldiers allowed to settle in the UK. Although he worked and voted against party policy, many constituents believed he took the right stance.
- Eventually, the government changed its policy on the issue.

Review and research

Should MPs be more representative of UK society in social and economic terms? How could this be achieved?
- The more socially representative MPs are, the more likely it is that Parliament will reflect the concerns of a wider cross-section of society.
- As more women MPs have been elected, so Parliament has paid greater attention to gender equality and family issues.
- As the number of MPs from ethnic minorities has slowly risen, ethnic minority communities have felt more able to use established channels via MPs to express their concerns.
- The number of MPs from different socio-economic groups depend on the decision made by local parties when they are selecting candidates, especially in areas where the party is likely to be successful.
- Labour has done this by insisting on all-woman shortlists in some areas.

- Younger MPs elected in 2005 included 25-year-old Jo Swinson, who won East Dunbartonshire for the Liberal Democrats and 32-year-old Stephen Crabb, who won Preseli Pembrokeshire for the Conservatives.
- At the next election younger MPs may be elected, since the minimum age for standing as a candidate has been reduced from 21 to 18, with Tony Benn's grand-daughter Emily Benn planning to stand as Labour candidate in Worthing East.

How effective are MPs?

- Most MPs work hard to represent their constituents diligently, regardless of party.
- If they support the government the most important thing is to turn up and vote to ensure that government policies are not defeated by opposition parties.
- In recent years MPs have played a bigger role in checking up on government departments through select committees – in the Treasury Select Committee, chaired by Labour MP John McFall, leading bankers were given a hard time, trying to justify their actions that contributed to the credit crunch.
- Constituents like to see their MPs asking questions, introducing private members' bills, arranging adjournment debates on matters of concern or generally participating in House of Commons' debates.
- But much of the work is undertaken far from the public gaze when MPs deal with correspondence, sit on standing committees (dealing with proposed new laws), and take part in party and all-party group meetings.

Should MPs be more independent of their parties?

- Parties are judged by their unity – the general public does not like a party to appear disunited.
- Most MPs contribute to policy formulation activities in their party and their ideas and suggestions will result in agreement being reached in most cases.
- If an MP disagrees with the party line, the general public like to see a show of independence – so the MP can publicly disagree.
- But if the government majority is small, 'unreliable' MPs who let the side down might find their local party has doubts about re-adopting them as a candidate for the next election unless the local party agrees with the stance taken by the MP.
- There has been a rather noticeable rise of cabinet government and reduction of influence of parliament, probably since the rise of Margaret Thatcher.

CITIZENSHIP STUDIES

Government

Lesson objectives	Specification link: Unit 1, Theme 2
By the end of this spread the student should: • understand key features of government in the UK, including the role of the Cabinet • recognise the importance, nature and activities of opposition parties	

Focus

...on the distinctions between government and opposition, ministers and civil servants, cabinet and shadow cabinets.

Key terms

• agencies

• cabinet

• executive

• government

• legislature

• opposition

• Permanent Secretary

• secretary of state or minister

• select committee

• shadow cabinet

Linked activity sheets

• The structure of government

Starter	Focus on the differences between Parliament and Government.
Development	Parliament is the House of Commons (elected) and House of Lords (appointed and hereditary) – it is the legislature (or law-making body) and includes all the members, regardless of political party.
	The Government (or executive) headed by the Prime Minister is made up of all the 100+ ministers appointed to run the government departments – Foreign Office, Home Office, Treasury, etc. – usually all members are drawn from the party with a majority in the House of Commons. Some are senior figures who meet together as the Cabinet (most senior 20+ ministers), others are more junior members in charge of just one part of a department's work. Opposition parties have shadow ministers to follow the work of each minister and department and act as the party's spokesperson.
	Senior civil servants (paid officials) assist ministers such as Lord Mandelson, Secretary of State for Business, Enterprise and Regulatory Reform (BERR) in policy making and the day-to-day running of a department (e.g. Sir Brian Bender as Permanent Secretary at the BERR Department). Much government work is undertaken by agencies that work exclusively on the delivery of a particular service – e.g. Prison Service agency – operating at arm's length but under the general guidance of the relevant ministry.
	The relationship between Prime Minister, Cabinet and Government can vary. Tony Blair is said to have made many decisions with close friends and then taken these decisions to the Cabinet to be simply

	noted, confirmed and implemented. Other Prime Ministers let the Cabinet make more of the decisions to operate a more collective form of decision-taking.
Plenary	Go over the *Checklist* points. Students could work on the *Further issues* questions as research or homework. Or you may want them to think about how a minister keeps Parliament informed of the activities of the department and how effectively Parliament monitors progress through Question Time and select committees.

Answers to questions in the Student Book

What's the issue?

Who belongs to Parliament but is not in the Government?
- The Government is the 100 or so ministers from the winning party, all of whom sit in the House of Commons as MPs or the House of Lords as peers.
- Sometimes all MPs or peers supporting the Government are loosely included in the term 'the Government', but this is not strictly correct.
- All other MPs and peers belong to Parliament but are not members of the Government.

Who works in the Government but is not in Parliament?
- All ministers will belong to either the House of Commons or the House of Lords and be members of the Government.
- They will be supported in their government departments by civil servants, including the most senior civil servant in each department - known as the permanent secretary - and also political advisers who support them in implementing party policy.
- Civil servants and political advisers work in the Government but only the ministers are in Parliament.

How is Government different from Parliament?
- Government is the executive function – it carries out the laws and makes decisions to deal with day-to-day situations such as a possible flu pandemic, the economic credit crunch or the problems caused by pirates operating off the coast of Somalia.
- Each year the Government publishes in the Queen's Speech the list of new laws it wants to have passed in the coming year as well as introducing a budget each year that may adjust taxes, pensions, etc.
- New laws, including the Finance Act, are considered as bills and then passed (or not passed) by Parliament in its role as the legislature (law-making body); this is a function separate and distinct from the executive function.

Margin questions

Do civil servants influence ministers too much?
This claim was often made before ministers appointed political advisers to help them implement the party manifesto on which they had been elected. It was believed that senior civil servants had a view of what needed to be done and promoted this point of view to new ministers (rather as in the comedy programme *Yes, Minister*). More recently, political advisers have often supported ministers to get a good political grounding before going on to become candidates and MPs themselves. The Conservative leader David Cameron was once a political adviser to Chancellor of the Exchequer Norman Lamont in the 1990s.

Review and research

Are key decisions made by the Prime Minister or by the whole Cabinet collectively?
The whole Cabinet involves 20 or so members – all senior ministers heading the most important departments of state. Different prime ministers adopt different styles and use the Cabinet in different ways. Some take most decisions themselves and then get them rubber-stamped by cabinet committees and the full Cabinet. Others may ask cabinet committees to work on particular problems and try to get the Cabinet to take the final decisions. Often governments must respond very quickly to situations (especially

CITIZENSHIP STUDIES

in days of 24-hour rolling news programmes) so many decisions may be decided by the Prime Minister and the relevant other minister.

Are decisions within ministries taken by ministers or civil servants?
- Formally decisions are taken by ministers.
- But a minister when first appointed may have little or no personal expertise in the department's work.
- In those circumstances – in the early days at least – a minister may listen carefully to advice from civil servants, including political advisers, before making a final decision.
- Ministers always need to be on top of their brief and a minister who does not fully understand the issues involved in a particular decision will quickly get into difficulties in answering questions in the House of Commons or a select committee or when participating in debates.

How could individuals persuade government to change their policies?
- Individuals who are members of the party in government could write to or go to see their MP, perhaps get the local branch of the party to pass a resolution on a matter of concern or go to a party conference and speak in favour of a change of policy.
- Individuals who are not in the same party as the government could campaign for a change of policy through their own party.
- People can also highlight the need for a changed policy through the media – asking questions on television programmes such as Radio 4's programme *Any Questions?* or BBC's programme *Question Time* or contributing to feedback programmes such as Radio 4's *Any Answers?* Or publishing a blog or sending emails to the websites of television and radio programmes.
- Individuals often turn to pressure groups to campaign for changes in policy and sometimes they will organise large-scale demonstrations. Such activities may demonstrate the strength of support for a particular cause but it is relatively rare that the government changes the direction of its policies as a result.
- Increasingly the government undertakes consultation exercises over policies so all individuals have an opportunity to express a point of view – such consultations are often undertaken via the internet and do sometimes lead to changes in policy.
- Individuals are encouraged by government to offer feedback on government policies – nowhere more so that the 10 Downing St website where (if people wish) they can start or sign up to a petition to the Prime Minister – http://petitions.number10.gov.uk/.

Legislation

Lesson objectives	Specification link: Unit 1, Theme 2
By the end of this spread the student should:
• know about different types of legislation and how they are initiated
• recognise the factors most likely to decide a bill's success
• understand the main stages of a bill becoming an Act of Parliament

Focus

...on public bills (bills promoted by Government or a backbench MP), private bills (promoted by private organisations such as universities, harbour authorities or railway companies to give limited powers in a particular area), delegated legislation (method of fast-tracking new rules under powers given to a minister by a previous Act of Parliament) and money bills (which unlike most other bills do not have to be approved by the House of Lords as well as the House of Commons).

Key terms

- delegated legislation (statutory instruments)
- government bills (public bills)
- money bills
- pressure groups

- private member's bills (public bills)
- private bills
- Royal Assent
- stages of a bill (first reading, second reading, committee stage, report stage, third reading)

Linked activity sheets

- How new laws are made

Starter	Start off with a Queen's Speech – the list of about 24 bills a government announces in October or November at the State Opening of Parliament and which it expects to put forward in the coming year.
Development	In addition there is a Finance Act every year to implement decisions announced in the Budget. Government bills are introduced first usually into the House of Commons but a few begin in the House of Lords. *It might be a good idea to record a Second Reading debate from BBC Parliament.*
	Government whips do their best to ensure their proposals are backed by all government supporters in both Houses, though neither Labour nor the Conservatives has an overall majority in the House of Lords (March 2009 membership – Lab 216, Con 197, Lib Dem 72, Non-party 244).
	The Labour Government was more successful in getting bills passed in the Commons than the Lords. All bills except money bills (or those rejected in Year 1 being re-presented in Year 2) have to be passed by both Houses.
	Many MPs and peers put forward private members' bills, often under a 'ten minute rule'. Few of these bills succeed but they gain publicity

	for the MP or peer who proposes them. Overall about 5 or 6 private member's bills are passed each session being considered mainly on Fridays.
	Private bills are not sponsored by MPs or peers but are a method for giving special powers to a railway company or an airport.
	Delegated legislation (statutory instruments) lay down precise rules for the implementation of a previously approved Act of Parliament.
Plenary	Go over the *Checklist* points. Students could work on the *Further issues* questions as research or homework. Or you may want them to evaluate the role of the House of Lords in the UK legislative system.

Answers to questions in the Student Book

What's the issue?

Why do backbench MPs sponsor legislation and why aren't they more successful?

- Many MPs put forward ten minute rule bills that enable them to speak for ten minutes in favour of a particular change in the law – such bills rarely make progress but they allow the MP some publicity and when the Government is drafting future bills it might include the MP's proposal.
- Backbench MPs have a better chance to get a law passed by entering a ballot – the first eight or so MPs to have their names drawn out of a ballot box have a reasonable chance of getting a law passed as long as it is not highly controversial and therefore is unlikely to provoke intense opposition from opponents.
- Whether an MP puts forward a ten minute rule bill or enters the annual ballot, she or he will want to promote a particular change in the law.
- Most MPs who are successful in changing the law do so with substantial help from pressure groups that encourage their members to press MPs from other constituencies to support the proposal.

Thousands of statutory instruments are passed every year. Why do you think this is?

- Most bills lay down general principles.
- Statutory instruments are needed to lay down specific rules in specific circumstances.
- If a law was passed about speed limits or railway stations, statutory instruments might be required later to spell out the details, e.g. which limits applied to which roads or what opening hours were appropriate to every railway station.

Are Private Acts of Parliament really needed?

- If a railway, harbour company, university or national park requires particular laws that would not apply in other places then the present way to achieve this is to promote a private bill.
- The procedure could be changed and a different method adopted to provide such laws, but sometimes circumstances do dictate that a particular situation can be resolved only by passing a new law, e.g. in exceptional circumstances, building a road across a cemetery.

Margin questions

Debates in the main chamber of the House of Commons are often poorly attended and not many MPs show up. What other work might MPs at Westminster be doing if they are not sitting in the chamber listening to a debate?

- The House of Commons will be full to bursting for Prime Minister's Question Time on Wednesdays and when the main speakers are introducing a key debate.
- For the rest of the time, a visit to BBC Parliament will confirm that only a small proportion of MPs are present for most debates – and most of those attending are MPs who either wish to speak on the matter or who have just spoken.
- MPs have a television feed to the House of Commons chamber in their offices so they can see what is taking place.
- They may receive up to 100 letters a day from constituents, government ministries and other organisations such as local councils, local businesses or voluntary bodies.
- Such correspondence needs to be answered and may cause the MP to take further action such as writing or speaking to a minister or putting down a question to a minister in the House of Commons.

- Constituents may also come to speak to their MP to seek advice or support over a particular problem.
- Many MPs are also assiduous in keeping their website up to date, so they need to speak to their staff in the constituency to ensure this happens.
- Apart from the main chamber of the House of Commons, debates and discussions take place in a second debating chamber in Westminster Hall and numerous committees also meet while the House of Commons is in session.
- If a vote is called (by ringing the division bell), MPs have eight minutes to get to the 'Yes' or 'No' lobby to vote and even though only a handful of members may have been in the chamber of the House of Commons, hundreds more suddenly appear from their offices, committee or meeting rooms, the House of Commons library or even the dining room.

Review and research

Should backbench MPs be allowed more time to get their own legislation passed?
If more time were allocated to legislation by backbench MPs there would be less time for government business. It is sometimes claimed that Government uses too much of Parliament's time. Although a case could be made to help backbench MPs pass more legislation (only 5 or 6 bills get passed in a typical year), there might be a stronger case for giving MPs sharper teeth to make ministers more accountable and to give select committees greater powers to check up on their activities. At present select committees produce authoritative reports but often these are given little consideration by the full House of Commons.

Are there enough safeguards when delegated legislation is passed?
There are both parliamentary and judicial safeguards over delegated legislation. Delegated legislation made by Statutory Instrument is either:
- approved by a vote of each House of Parliament before it is made, or
- subject to a veto by either House within a certain period after it is made.

Judicial control is exercised through the means of judicial review. Because delegated legislation is made by a person exercising a power given by an Act of Parliament for a particular purpose, it can be struck down by the courts if they conclude that the order goes beyond the scope of the enabling law on which it is based.

Could the process of making laws be simpler?
- If the first reading of a bill is about the general idea and the second reading considers its range and principles, the committee stage is important because this is where most detailed consideration is given.
- Changes made in committee are reported (report stage) and then the House needs to decide whether it will accept the version the committee has presented (third reading).
- Since Parliament is made up of both the House of Commons and the House of Lords, the bill then needs to go through the same procedure in the other House.
- Although one party usually has a majority in the House of Commons, this is not the case in the House of Lords so approval in this House could indicate how far the bill could be acceptable to the wider public.
- It may sound long and complicated but a law could result in a person going to prison if they do not obey, so it is important that it is passed in a form that is both fair and workable and likely to meet the problem it was intended to resolve.

Active participation: Influencing decisions

Lesson objectives	Specification link: Unit 1, Theme 2
By the end of this spread the student should: • be able to discuss pressure groups, consultation and the role of the voluntary sector • recognise that actions by individuals and groups lead to policy proposals, debates and outcomes • understand the strength and importance of public opinion locally and nationally	

Focus

...on the idea of choice. Locally, nationally and internationally, decisions involve choices – a council may have to decide whether to rebuild its town centre or to build a new estate of houses because it probably can't afford to do both; a government may want to build eco-towns but where? Final decisions are taken after individuals and groups have had their say. Often, protesters who want an eco-town built at A instead of B may be balanced by other groups that favour B instead of A!

Key terms

• charities
• consultation
• Crossrail
• eco-town

• 'insider' and 'outsider' pressure groups
• 'not in my backyard' – 'NIMBY'
• voluntary bodies/voluntary work
• wind farm

Linked activity sheets

• Peace one day
• Launch your own pressure group

Starter	Start with wind farms. Would students object to proposals to build a wind farm near their homes? Introduce NIMBY idea. Should a council approve a wind farm (since green energy is needed) and over-rule you?
Development	Then discuss Crossrail. Building it will cause massive disruption but there are long-term benefits to London. Should those who said it would cause too much chaos have been allowed to win the day? *If people's views are going to be ignored, why ask them in the first place?* People's views are taken seriously and often result in policies being changed or withdrawn altogether – e.g. the proposed badger cull in 2008. The building of new towns such as Milton Keynes should remind us that, while the plans went ahead, serious efforts were made to overcome the objections of protesters so the final outcome was improved for everyone. Make sure students understand what pressure groups are and the distinction between 'insider' and 'outsider' groups. 'Insider' groups have technical expertise and Government listens carefully to their points; 'outsider' groups generally offer a different point of view and therefore try to mobilise public opinion through publicity stunts,

	petitions or demonstrations.
	Campaigning for or against change can be undertaken by organisations that feel strongly about proposals – so a sports or religious group or a charity may join a campaign if it has a point of view to express.
	Don't underestimate the importance of voluntary bodies – if they support a particular cause, many others will do so also because such groups are highly respected in the community.
Plenary	Go over the *Checklist* points. Students could work on the *Further issues* questions as research or homework. Or you may want them to find out the latest information on wind farm, eco-town and Crossrail developments.

Answers to questions in the Student Book

What's the issue?

When might a charity, religious group or sports club act as a pressure group, trying to change government policy?
- A charity may be affected by government policies, e.g. tax treatment of charities.
- A religious group may have views about a particular aspect of government policy, e.g. people other than Muslim girls at schools should have a veil.
- A sports club may be affected by government tax or sport policies or rules governing licensed bars at match venues.
- If these groups are affected by government proposals to change a policy or if they want to see an existing policy change, they may try to mobilise support for their point of view by acting like a pressure group.

Can you think of other 'insider' groups?
- Whether a group is an 'insider' group or not will depend partly on a Government's attitude to a group.
- Trade unions are more obviously 'insiders' so far as Labour is concerned, but it is less likely their views would be valued if a very right-wing Government was in office (e.g. Mrs Thatcher's Governments in 1980s).
- Nonetheless both Labour and Conservative Governments would tend to regard trade unions and business organisations as 'insiders' as well as respected groups with specific, technical knowledge such as Amnesty International or the Royal Society for the Protection of Birds (RSPB).

Can you think of other 'outsider' groups?
- Groups with which a Government disagrees will usually not sustain 'insider' status for long. While the Labour Government has been in office, the pro-hunting Countryside Alliance has been an 'outsider' group; this would possibly not be the case if a Conservative Government took office. Another 'outsider' group in the UK is the 'Legalise Cannabis Alliance'.

Margin questions

How much does the attention given to a group and whether it is seen as an 'insider' or 'outsider' depend on the government itself rather than the group?
As indicated above, some groups are too important to ignore and have technical information and communication channels that no Government would wish to ignore. But for the rest, the Government will not be interested in hearing from groups that are at odds with their own objectives on most issues so they will be treated as 'outsiders'. The Countryside Alliance could potentially become an 'insider' group if a Conservative Government were to be elected.

Is the majority always right even if they are behaving selfishly or have not fully taken the 'big picture' into account?
In reality in a country with 40 million adults, most groups represent minorities. Governments are elected to do what they consider right, taking everything into account. It would be wrong for them to adopt a

policy they believed mistaken simply because an opinion poll indicated majority support for it. Of course, if the issue had been the subject of a referendum, a Government or local government would probably have no option but to accept the verdict of the voters.

Review and research

Should official bodies ever go against the wishes of large numbers of protesters?

Official bodies in a democracy have to act on the policies for which they have a mandate. Protesters may make them reconsider their commitment to particular policies (e.g. the 'poll tax' in the early 1990s) but generally even large numbers of protesters may be a minority. After all, who is to say that there are not as many or more supporters for a policy as those who turn out to protest? In some areas, large numbers of people have turned out to protest against the construction of a new wind farm, yet few people doubt such wind farms are desirable and that it is in the national interest for them to be built.

Should the needs or opinions of businesses count for more than voluntary bodies, religious groups or sports clubs?

- Businesses are important as employers and wealth-creators but many would say they are no more important than voluntary bodies (often do much good as charities), religious groups (moral welfare), and sports clubs (provide leisure interests).
- Businesses themselves do want their voice and their concerns to be heard but people who work in the businesses often also support charities, churches and sports clubs so would not wish such bodies to be ignored or excluded from consideration.

Do interests matter as much or more than opinions?

- An interest may involve someone's livelihood or property or health. Against such things opinions can sometimes appear quite frivolous – yet in fact interests are expressed as opinions.
- The worker at a firm will oppose its closure if it could mean losing his or her job. Yet if the worker retrains and gets another job he may be able to improve his career.
- If someone is personally affected in a material way by a policy we can say the person has a 'self-interest'.
- But it may not be right to see 'self-interest' on the part of some people as a good reason to make or change policy.
- A person may not want an extra carriageway to be added to a road in front of her house because she may not like the noise of traffic or the fact that she will lose some of her garden, but it may add to road safety overall.

Campaigning for or against change

Lesson objectives	Specification link: Unit 1, Theme 2
By the end of this spread the student should: • understand the ways in which citizens can seek to mobilise opinion • recognise that demonstrations and petitions express opinions but often do not lead to change • know about local and national referendums	

Focus

...on the greater openness in today's society and changes in technology which mean individuals or groups can quickly spread their ideas to millions – with fewer people belonging to political parties and more people joining pressure groups, it becomes all the more difficult to make decisions.

Key terms

- Anti-Poll Tax demonstration
- e-petitions (e.g. on 10 Downing St website)
- 'immediate news'
- Iraq war

- 'liberty and livelihood' campaign
- referendums
- weblogs (blogs)

Linked activity sheets

- Peace one day
- Launch your own pressure group

Starter	Get the students thinking about the Internet and other technologies such as mobile phones – what can they do to communicate and share ideas that people couldn't do 20 years ago?
Development	Discuss how sites such as *Facebook* make it so much easier to spread ideas. Then go to the website of a newspaper such as *The Independent* and look at the comments readers have added to their news stories – students should recognise this as a sort of developing 'national conversation'. Does easy access to the Internet (especially with broadband) give people more opportunities to support campaigns they favour rather than joining a political party to do the campaigning for them? *So do we need to hold demonstrations any more?* Yes. They may not change a Government's mind (though the Anti-Poll Tax demonstrations did achieve that in the early 1990s) but they show how much support particular causes have and may encourage some people who had been sitting on the fence to give their support. Referendums allow people to say 'Yes' or 'No' in answer to a specific policy question – sometimes referendums are held (as in 1975) when a Government is split on an issue as Harold Wilson's Government was over Europe.

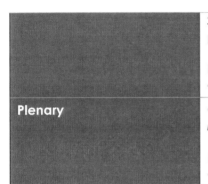

	Social networking sites can play an enormous part in persuading people whether or how to vote in elections and referendums. In the USA, Barack Obama largely bypassed formal party procedures by building a loyal Internet army and keeping in close touch with them all throughout his campaign for the presidency in 2008.
Plenary	Go over the *Checklist* points. Students could work on the *Further issues* questions as research or homework. Or they could go on the Internet and look to see what campaigns are being promoted by local MPs or by pressure groups such as Human Rights Watch, Liberty or environmental groups such as those listed on SB p. 68.

Answers to questions in the Student Book

What's the issue?

What are the advantages and disadvantages of today's 'immediate news'?
- Needing to maintain programmes for 24 hours a day, rolling news programmes mean that the news agenda has to move on continually.
- Before such programmes were shown politicians could repeat the same speech many times whereas now they want a different sound bite a day if any attention is to be paid to them.
- On the other hand, some people believe that, with so much time to fill, news broadcasters focus on issues in great depth and can sometimes be accused of exaggerating or causing moral panics.

Has the Internet really made individuals and groups more powerful?
- The Internet is undoubtedly an easy source of information for individuals.
- It also gives individuals power because they can offer comments of their own and thus contribute to shaping the news agenda.
- This also means individuals can communicate in web-rooms and blogs to form pressure groups.

Why have pressure group memberships risen as the number of political party memberships has gone down?
- With access to so much information via the Internet, many people are more aware of particular issues and causes and now have a resource for supporting the campaigns to which they are most attracted.
- Perhaps this is why pressure group memberships have risen sharply.
- Working through a political party may not always the best way to promote a cause, particularly if a party is out of power locally and/or nationally.

Review and research

Do demonstrations change public opinion?
A well-attended demonstration may show that a particular campaign has considerable support and give more people confidence that they should join it too.
Such changes in public opinion are often reflected in subsequent local and national elections.
However, a demonstration often does not move a government to change its mind, e.g. demonstrations against the Iraq war in 2003.

Is the public given enough information to decide issues in referendums?
- If an issue is very complicated, it might be difficult to put over all the arguments on both sides.
- Researchers have suggested that decisions taken by voters in referendums in various countries are no better (or worse) than decisions taken by legislators.
- Most of the time, choices are quite simple and the campaigns produce information that goes into as much depth as voters require, varying from quick summary to detailed analysis.
- To argue that voters are ill equipped to participate in referendums would be a serious threat to the whole idea and legitimacy of referendums.

Are people now better able to participate because of the Internet and the media?

- Blogging, texting, emailing and phone-ins to radio and television programmes all mean people have many more ways in which they can choose to participate – something that increasing numbers of people now do.

Decision-making in the UK and beyond: Local and regional forms of government in the UK

Lesson objectives	Specification link: Unit 1, Theme 2

By the end of this spread the student should:

- understand that councils provide local democracy, deliver a wide range of services and are sometimes led by elected mayors

- recognise that central government has devolved many powers to the Scottish Parliament, the Welsh Assembly and the Northern Ireland Assembly

- know that while the UK is usually run by a majority government, the devolved bodies (elected by PR) are usually controlled by no one party, resulting in minority or coalition governments

Focus

...on how councillors support local democracy and the difference they can make to decisions finally taken – e.g. choices over whether to spend money on a leisure centre or a new theatre (if both cannot be afforded) or over which school to close (as numbers of children in an area decrease).

Key terms

- coalition, minority and majority governments
- councils/ council services, e.g. education, environmental health, fire, highways, libraries, police, social services, trading standards, waste management
- council budgets/council tax
- devolution/devolved powers, e.g. education, health, personal social care, rural affairs, tourism and transport

- elected mayors
- merged councils, e.g. Kirklees, Herefordshire
- Northern Ireland Assembly
- Scottish Parliament
- Welsh Assembly

Linked activity sheets

- Heart transplant

Starter	Start with the paradox – councils are getting bigger (more streamlined/efficient?), but central government is slimming down, devolving some of its powers to new bodies in Scotland, Wales and Northern Ireland to give people more say over their own affairs.
Development	Although Herefordshire and Kirklees are discussed, use examples in your own area – let the students think about advantages and disadvantages of such changes. Is it better to have an elected mayor as chief policy maker or to leave that to elected councillors? An elected mayor can make a big difference – Ken Livingstone as Mayor of London was very different from Boris Johnson in policy terms as well as style.
	Scots, Welsh and Northern Irish people now decide more of their own affairs but there are significant differences over policies in the different countries – e.g. over personal social care, prescription charges and student fees at university – is this good or bad? Largely

	because the devolved bodies are elected by PR, no one party has an overall majority – at first there was a Liberal Democrat/Labour coalition in Scotland, which was replaced in 2007 by a minority Scots Nat/Green government – make sure the students understand the difference between a minority and a coalition government.
Plenary	Go over the *Checklist* points. Students could work on the *Further issues* questions as research or homework. Or you may want them to consider the choices councils have to make – to go for the lowest budget/council tax possible or to provide more services even if council tax has to rise as a result.

Answers to questions in the Student Book

What's the issue?

Do local people have enough chance to *make a difference* with the new larger local authorities?
- The argument is that larger units are more efficient – but local activists sometimes question whether this also means less democratic.
- However, larger councils often have sub-committees covering activities in particular locations, and these do give some autonomy to local members to address purely local concerns.
- Local elections do give individuals, local parties and national parties the opportunity to participate in elections as well as campaigning through local groups if they so wish.

How does combining councils make services more efficient and cost-effective?
- If there used to be ten councils each with separate buildings, specialist officers, equipment, lists of meetings etc., it should make sense on grounds of economies of scale to concentrate them so there are fewer buildings in use, fewer specialist officers employed and a central set of equipment so that, for example, ten lots of computing or printing equipment are not required.
- There could then also be fewer meetings and fewer councillors overall.

Has the 'local' been taken out of 'local government'?
To some extent yes – except that communications are now much better than they used to be. Use of telephone, Internet and video can mean all local residents in a council area such as Herefordshire or Kirklees can use local offices or the Internet to get just as good a service as or better than they used to enjoy with a multitude of smaller councils

Margin questions

What is the ideal population size for delivering a service such as education, fire, police or social services?
Different studies have produced different figures but the essential fact is that such services work best if they have a minimum population of 250,000 to justify the employment of specialist teams on which high quality services depend. Sometimes services such as police are organised by providing one service covering more than one local authority area, e.g. there is just one police service covering Shropshire, Herefordshire and Worcestershire, known as the West Mercia Police Force.

Is there a reason why the devolved bodies (Northern Ireland, Wales and Scotland) all lack majority governments? What are the advantages or disadvantages of this?
In the 2005 general election Labour had clear majorities in the House of Commons from Scotland (Lab 41, Lib Dem 11, SNP 6, Con 1) and Wales (Lab 29, Lib Dem 4, Plaid Cymru 3, Con 3) but in the elections for the Scottish Parliament and the Welsh Assembly the balance of parties was very different because, instead of using the first-past-the-post electoral system, a system of proportional representation was used. Supporters of single majority government where one party is in charge would deplore the make-up of the devolved bodies. Those who favour the coalition and minority government administrations in Belfast, Cardiff and Edinburgh would probably point out that multi-party government gives close scrutiny of issues and appears to have resulted in perfectly workable government.

CITIZENSHIP STUDIES

Review and research

What are the strengths and weaknesses of having elected mayors?

An elected mayor is a figurehead who can make crucial decisions, working with councillors rather than leaving them to make decisions on their own. The most famous elected mayor serves London – first Ken Livingstone, then Boris Johnson. Other towns such as Torbay (Conservative) and Watford (Lib Dem) have also chosen to go over to the 'elected mayor' model in which councillors are downgraded. The advantage of the system is to have someone who is clearly heading up decision-making. The disadvantage is that elected councillors representing local residents have less say and influence.

Does it matter if different policies apply in England, Wales and Scotland?

- Once Scotland and Wales are allowed to make decisions for themselves, there is no reason why the decisions made by their administrations should be the same as the Government's decisions for England – this has been seen over matters such as university top-up fees, prescription charges and personal care arrangements for the infirm.
- It might seem consistent to operate uniform policies but if different communities have different priorities, why not?

What are the advantages and disadvantages of having majority, coalition or minority governments

- If a Government knows it has an overall majority then it knows it can get any policy through Parliament as long as it keeps the support of all its MPs – there is certainty about what is going to happen.
- But a Government with a secure majority can become lazy, assume that whatever ideas it has will be passed and therefore sometimes puts forward proposals that are not as well researched and considered as they should be – causing some of their own MPs to become restive and possibly rebel.
- In a minority government situation, the Government has fewer than half the seats in the Parliament and therefore must find partners to support its proposals. Thus the SNP/Green minority government in 2009 can get its policies accepted only if it wins support from one or more other parties (they may be backed by Lib Dems on one policy, Conservatives on a second and possibly Labour on a third). Such a system results in issues being hotly debated and politicians have to work hard to find a consensus on which sufficient members will agree.
- In a coalition government, two or more parties come together and work as a government on the basis of an agreement. Both parties will have determined which of their members fill ministerial posts and there will be an agreed policy programme on which the two parties will both work. Wales has seen Lib Dem/Labour coalition government, Labour minority government and Lab/Plaid Cymru coalition government since it was formed. Issues must still be closely debated but the existence of a coalition agreement does offer a degree of certainty.

CITIZENSHIP STUDIES

Government beyond the UK

Lesson objectives	Specification link: Unit 1, Theme 2
By the end of this spread the student should: • be aware of presidential forms of government such as those in France or the USA • know about democratic and non-democratic forms of government in other countries	

Focus

...on the roles of head of state and head of government – in the UK, Her Majesty the Queen and the Prime Minister. In the USA President Obama fills both roles. France and Russia have both a president and a prime minister. Countries such as North Korea and Zimbabwe claim to be democratic republics but this is not a form of democracy UK citizens would recognise as such.

Key terms

• Congress (USA) – Senate and House of Representatives

• democratic republic (North Korea)

• electoral college (USA)

• executive (government)

• head of government

• head of state

• legislature (law-makers)

• National Assembly (France)

• president

• prime minister

Starter	What does it mean to be a head of government and a head of state? Should a head of state be an impartial non-controversial figure (such as HM the Queen)? What problems might arise if someone has to fill both roles (e.g. the US president)?
Development	Whether a country has one person in both roles elected via an electoral college (as in the USA) or political figures in both roles (as in France), there is no question of their commitment to democracy – though it may take a slightly different form from our own. Countries such as Zimbabwe have elaborate ceremonies with soldiers in uniforms yet the government under President Robert Mugabe hung on to office in a cruel, dishonest and cynical fashion. North Korea has elections and describes itself as a 'democratic republic' yet there is only one party and no democratic freedom. Russia has elections but democracy is limited because some candidates are not allowed to stand for office if they might challenge the regime. Commonwealth countries such as Canada, Australia, India, Malta, South Africa and New Zealand have established democratic procedures – other countries such as Pakistan and Kenya are committed to the idea of democracy but their systems have been challenged in recent years.
Plenary	Go over the *Checklist* points. Students could work on the *Further issues* questions as research or homework. Or you may want them to examine the relationship between people, living standards and government in a range of countries with a non-democratic form of government.

Answers to questions in the Student Book

What's the issue?

Is it better for the head of state to be a neutral and non-controversial figure?
- HM The Queen is an impartial person acting as head of state above the battle between parties – this is the UK model.
- In France and the USA the presidency is occupied by a person elected on a party label and seen as controversial.
- To some extent US presidents speak for the nation at times of crisis even though elected on a partisan basis.

Is it better for a head of government to be elected separately (as US and French presidents are) – from elections for Congress (USA) or the National Assembly (France)?
- Both systems are democratic but different, and match the view of democracy in the respective countries.
- Barack Obama was elected in 2008 as the USA's chief executive and head of government as well as being elected head of state.
- The US presidency covers both roles.
- The leader of the largest party in the UK House of Commons is called upon by the Queen to become Prime Minister and head of government.
- Similarly the French President appoints the French Prime Minister.
- If the UK model operated in the US or France, the head of government would be the head of the majority party in the Congress or the National Assembly.

Is the UK model better in which the Prime Minister and head of government holds the office because his party has majority support in the House of Commons?
- In the USA the president fills both roles: if a president dies or resigns, the system allows for a new person (the vice president) to assume the office and replace the former holder until the next due election.
- In the USA party discipline is weaker than in the UK so the idea of a firm, consistent party majority in either the House of Representatives or the Senate is unlikely – members vote as they think their constituents would want them to and they often do not back their own party.
- In the UK it is possible to transfer power – Gordon Brown replaced Tony Blair when he resigned but if Gordon Brown were to lose too many votes in the House of Commons he might be expected to resign and call a general election so a new government could be elected.
- In the USA presidential elections are held on fixed dates every four years. The UK has fixed dates for elections to the European Parliament and the devolved bodies but not to Westminster.

Review and research

If a country treats its people badly, should other countries get involved? If so, what should they do?
Each country is supposed to be sovereign, running its own affairs without interference from others. In democratic countries, a poor government can be turned out of office and replaced by a better one. But in non-democratic countries (e.g. Burma/Myanmar), dictators may seize and hold on to power and are reluctant to relinquish it. Other countries may try to impose economic sanctions to put pressure on unsatisfactory leaders but they are often rebuffed by claims from the country that the management of their country is their concern alone. Human rights organisations sometimes suggest that concern for humanity overrides issues of sovereignty and the internal integrity of individual countries, though UN peacekeepers have intervened in trouble spots where civil wars and allegations of genocide have been made in former Yugoslavia, Sierra Leone and DR Congo. However, there still exists debate whether other countries should become involved.

Which other countries have a good system of democracy and what ideas could we borrow from them to add to our own system of democracy?
- Systems of government have to fit in with the culture of each country where they operate.
- A system that is highly regarded and accepted in one country might not be accepted or effective elsewhere.
- Apart from the head of government/head of state distinction discussed above, some countries have fixed term Parliaments and a variety of electoral systems is used.

- Some countries have many more referendums than we do, giving voters the opportunity to veto a proposed Act of Parliament if they so wish or 'recall' public officials such as MPs if their behaviour becomes unacceptable.
- Since 1951 New Zealand has had only one 'house' of its Parliament which is unicameral.
- In the USA the 50 states have much greater powers in their own right than the UK has allowed so far to the devolved administrations in Wales, Scotland and Northern Ireland.

Where would you place Commonwealth countries on a democratic 'order of merit'?

- A set of criteria would need to be decided, of which fair elections and acceptance of results and peaceful transition of government from one party to another would seem of paramount importance.
- Such conditions are met in countries such as India, Australia, New Zealand, Malta and Canada but are less evident in Kenya and Zimbabwe (no longer a member of the Commonwealth).

CITIZENSHIP STUDIES

Saving our world:
Global warming and sustainability

Lesson objectives	Specification link: Unit 1, Theme 3
By the end of this spread the student should: • understand the reasons for global warming and climate change • recognise the significance of renewable and non-renewable energy sources • understand the possible consequences of global warming and how they might be reduced	

Focus

…on why some people may take the prospect of global warming much less seriously than others, resist the changes needed to alleviate the problems identified by scientists and see the problem as something over which others should take action.

Key terms

- carbon emissions
- climate change
- fossil fuels
- global warming

- greenhouse gases
- nuclear power
- renewable/non-renewable energy
- sustainability

Linked activity sheets

- How green is your school?
- Eco-bingo

Starter	From science or geography and wider reading or viewing, all students should be familiar with the key terms – brainstorm their meanings and importance on the board/screen.
Development	Ask the students how the potential dangers could lead to the developments listed in the 'Possible consequences' section. Set up a mini-debate – is it too late to take action (so we should do nothing) or will things only get worse if we do nothing? What alternative sources of energy might be introduced that involve less potential damage to the environment – work through the pie chart on p. 92 – look at each usage in turn: Industry Transport Power stations Land use Waste disposal Agriculture Fossil fuel processing Residential and commercial In what sense is nuclear power a non-renewable form of energy? So why is government planning to build nuclear power stations? (The supply of uranium is finite but nuclear power stations do not produce greenhouse gases. However, others say nuclear waste presents different but very real and long-term dangers.)

CITIZENSHIP STUDIES

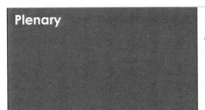

Plenary	Go over the *Checklist* points. Students could work on the *Further issues* questions as research or homework. Or you may want them to consider why some people oppose the development of wind farms in an area while others want to see many more developed – some students could do a survey of the number of wind turbines or solar panels in their area.

Answers to questions in the Student Book

What's the issue?

If global warming is really taking place, will it seriously affect our future?
It could cause wildlife to move on, some lands nearer the equator could turn to desert, seasons and weather would change, Britain's coastline could become unrecognisable as a result of raised sea levels, some towns could completely disappear, new plants could be seen in Britain and mosquitoes could thrive in Britain, bringing a danger of malaria.

Should we be concerned about, or simply ignore, the possible effects of global warming?
- Scientists believe the changes we are now seeing result from carbon emissions building up since the earliest days of the industrial revolution in Europe and the US in the 18th and 19th centuries.
- But considerable progress has already been made in achieving clean air.
- If nothing is done, things would undoubtedly get worse.
- If we try to reduce greenhouse gas emissions, we may avoid the worst of the changes that could otherwise occur.
- New technologies to tackle global warming may have an overall beneficial effect on people's lifestyles.

Margin questions

Which human activities are most likely to produce greenhouse gases?
- Driving a car (unless it runs on hydrogen or electricity from renewable energy)
- Burning a coal fire
- Converting iron ore into manufactured iron and steel
- Using electricity (if it is generated from fossil fuels)
- Cutting down rainforests.

What are some possible problems that may happen in 50 years' time?
- Non-renewable forms of energy such as coal and oil lead to carbon emissions which lead to global warming and climate change.
- If new technologies can develop alternative sources of power, then we won't need coal and oil in future.
- However, if strategies such as 'clean coal' and 'carbon capture' are adopted, then the diminution of a finite supply of a particular material could become very significant.
- If more parts of Africa become virtually uninhabitable, where will the local populations move to?
- How will these populations be fed and how will they earn a living?
- As temperatures rise, some forms of farming may seek to move north to cooler climates. With global warming come water shortages.
- A major cause of carbon emissions is travel by air – unless new technologies can be created so that planes can use biofuels, air travel may need to be heavily restricted; prices could rise tenfold to encourage passengers to turn to other forms of travel.

Review and research

How does the media present global warming?
The parts of the media that in the past have received much advertising from the oil and motor industries have been keen to suggest that global warming is a lot of fuss about nothing. They pick up the claims of climate change deniers that the whole problem is linked to natural (not man-made) phenomena. They claim the sun's magnetic field and the solar wind modulate the amount of high energy cosmic radiation that

CITIZENSHIP STUDIES

the earth receives, thus affecting the low altitude cloud cover and the amount of water vapour in the atmosphere, which regulating the climate. Other parts of the media see the dangers of global warming as a race against time, drawing on the kind of analysis shown in Al Gore's film *An Inconvenient Truth*. With the election of President Obama and the departure of President Bush, the urgent need to address climate change as a man-made development has moved up several gears. The media tends to be negative, stressing the bad news, but there is progress and good news on some issues, too.

Are older people as concerned about global warming as younger people?

- Some older people feel that their generation has made things worse for future generations and that they are morally obliged to try to help put things right.
- Others feel that the discovery and investment in new technologies is a problem for their children since global warming is unlikely to make much difference to them personally in their remaining years of life.

How can you help to raise awareness and a willingness to take positive action?

- The change in opinion over the past few years shows that the dangers of carbon emissions leading to climate change can be tackled.
- The sense of urgency felt by many people in the UK and other countries has driven the Government to set a target of reducing such emissions by 80% by 2050.
- By embracing new technologies, emphasising sustainability, turning to renewable energy, saving energy use wherever possible (e.g. home insulation and recycling), we can all contribute to a reduction in greenhouse gas emissions.

What can be done?

Lesson objectives	Specification link: Unit 1, Theme 3
By the end of this spread the student should: • know how individuals can make a difference through waste disposal, recycling and shared car schemes • recognise how new approaches to transport and commuting could help reduce greenhouse gases • understand how changes in business practices and council initiatives could cut emissions of greenhouse gases	

Focus

...on how changes in waste disposal, recycling, shared car schemes, congestion charging and greater use of public transport can go a long way to tackle the problem of climate change.

Key terms

• commuting

• congestion

• congestion charge

• energy efficiency

• hybrid cars

• insulation

• NIMBY – not in my backyard

• public transport

• recycling

• walking bus

Linked activity sheets

• Individuals and change

• How green is your school?

• Eco-bingo

Starter	Begin with how the students got to school – Who walked? Who cycled? Who used a bus? Who came in a car? Who shared the car journey with others? How could the energy use have been cut – and kept everyone safe at the same time – e.g. could the walkers have formed a 'walking bus'?
Development	Discuss how changes could cut energy use and reduce global warming: • Less landfill, more incineration and recycling • Less packaging on goods we buy in the supermarket • Home insulation and not leaving televisions or computers on standby • Using energy efficient light bulbs. Find an example of a NIMBY activity (e.g. opposing a local wind farm development) in your area – or find a recent one elsewhere. Ask the students why the opponents might take the view they do? • Is NIMBYism selfish?

	• Do NIMBY campaigners not understand the dangers of global warming?
	• Is it right to override the wishes of the individual opponents?
	Discuss public transport. Has congestion charging reduced congestion? How could public transport be improved, so more people use buses, trains and trams and what benefit would this bring in terms of congestion, saving time and reducing pollution?
Plenary	Go over the *Checklist* points. Students could work on the *Further issues* questions as research or homework. Or you may want them to think about actions their family has taken in recent years to cut energy use – and what further changes they could make.

Answers to questions in the Student Book

What's the issue?

Is burning fossil fuels the major cause of the increasing amount of CO_2 in the atmosphere?
- Burning fossil fuels is undoubtedly a major cause of more carbon dioxide and other greenhouse gases such as methane being in the atmosphere.
- But don't forget that accumulations of carbon dioxide in the atmosphere can also come with the cutting down of rainforest on the other side of the planet.
- Methane seeping from landfill sites and animal waste can also be a major cause of greenhouse gases, as can other natural sources of carbon dioxide unrelated to human activities.

How can road congestion, and the pollution it brings, be reduced?
- In cities such as London and Durham, congestion charging has encouraged more people to use public transport or to walk or cycle (which is both healthier and cheaper).
- Better public transport services have encouraged many people to give up their cars in favour of trams, trains and buses.
- Pollution from cars and other vehicles can be reduced by setting new standards for vehicle emissions – the price of a car tax disc is now related to how clean its emissions are.
- More people are turning towards electric-powered or hybrid cars.

Why do NIMBY groups oppose efforts to improve the environment?
- Individuals who want to protect the view from their window may oppose the building of wind farms or nuclear power stations.
- They may claim that such developments would reduce the value of their property and their enjoyment of it.
- But if their activities lead to continued burning of fossil fuels and slow down the development of non-renewable forms of energy, they could be accused of being selfish – and those who heeded their opposition might be considered irresponsible.
- However, those campaigning against mobile phone masts may not be NIMBY, but environmentalists, too.

Margin questions

Has the government done anything to encourage congestion charging in cities?
Environmental groups such as Friends of the Earth have complained that the Government has been too timid in promoting charging schemes to reduce traffic congestion. Although the London and Durham schemes are generally regarded as successful, similar local schemes proposed for Edinburgh and Manchester were rejected by 74% to 26% and 79% to 21% respectively.

Has congestion charging reduced the number of car journeys in cities like London and Durham?
The results are controversial and difficult to measure. However, *Transport for London*'s 2007 report found that the level of traffic of all vehicle types entering the central Congestion Charge Zone was consistently 16% lower in 2006 than the pre-charge levels in 2002.

CITIZENSHIP STUDIES

Review and research

How can we be more energy efficient in our homes?

Solar panels, wind turbines, heat exchangers and other innovations can increase the amount of renewable energy we use. We can insulate our homes so less energy is lost through windows and roof spaces. We can stop leaving televisions and computers on standby and replace existing light bulbs with energy efficient ones. We can ensure old newspapers, cardboard, plastics and tins go to be recycled.

What can be done to make school more environmentally friendly?

- Many schools now have their own wind turbines and solar panels, are committed to recycling and energy conservation and organise car-sharing and walking bus schemes to get pupils to school safely yet with least energy use.
- The government is committed to rebuilding many schools and the designs of new buildings can be much more energy efficient than the premises they replace.
- Good practice in schools can ensure pupils are environmentally aware of the consequences of their actions in later life as adults.

How well does your local council publicise energy saving initiatives?

Sounds like a worthwhile project for Units 2 or 4!

Solutions to global problems

Lesson objectives	Specification link: Unit 1, Theme 3
By the end of this spread the student should: • know about public attitudes and the nature, successes and impact of campaigns by environmental groups • recognise the nature of international efforts to combat global warming • understand the role of councils, including Local Agenda 21	

Focus

...on the problem of getting developing countries (which mostly haven't caused massive carbon emissions over the past 250 years) to agree to the same sorts of target as those applying to developed countries (who did do most of the damage, albeit probably unknowingly until recently).

Key terms

• developed and developing countries

• green taxes

• Kyoto, Rio de Janeiro & Copenhagen summits

• Local agenda 21

• Pressure groups – e.g. Greenpeace

• sustainable development

Linked activity sheets

• How green is your school?

• Eco-bingo

Starter	Why do environmental campaigners favour road pricing/congestion charging? To put people off driving into cities or using cars for longer journeys instead of public transport.
Development	Look at the case for green taxes.
	What else would environmentalists like to stop people doing? If these things were taxed, would this put people off doing them?
	When people tell pollsters they oppose more 'green laws' is this because they don't understand the seriousness of the situation or because they don't like changing their behaviour?
	Instead of trying to persuade people to stop using the standby mode on televisions or computers, should such products not be built with this facility in future?
	Introduce the idea of Local Agenda 21 (acting locally, thinking globally). Find out how your local council has embraced/acted on this scheme.
	Check on the UN website to see how the global warming agenda has changed since the Kyoto Agreement in 1992.
	Why did the USA under President Bush fail to take global warming seriously?
	Why – and how - has President Obama in the USA used the economic downturn to make US car companies focus on building smaller, cheaper cars that are more energy efficient?

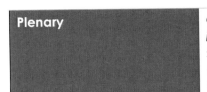

Plenary	Go over the *Checklist* points. Students could work on the *Further issues* questions as research or homework. Or you may want them to spend some time exploring how more people could be made aware of climate change dangers – and what they could do to reduce the carbon emissions for which they and their family are responsible.

Answers to questions in the Student Book

What's the issue?

Is a cartoon more effective than an opinion poll as a way of drawing attention to an issue like global warming?
- Both can be effective.
- A cartoon may give people a laugh but they will often take on board the underlying point – it may help them recognise the need to change their own behaviour.

What does the opinion poll research tell you about attitudes to the environment?
- Opinion polls overall show that more people recognise the importance of green issues – especially younger, more educated people.
- There are still some 'climate change deniers' but not as many as previously.
- People generally don't want higher taxes, whether green taxes or other taxes, yet sometimes it is recognised that a tax can help to change behaviour.
- Some campaigners for green taxes propose that, if more money were raised in this way, much less would need to be collected in traditional ways, allowing the standard rate of income tax to be cut by 20% to 16p in £.

Why do you think men might oppose green legislation more than women?
- Many men earn more than women and so pay more in tax.
- Many men give their car and driving a higher priority than women do.
- Perhaps this explains why the idea of being taxed more on a high powered car or reducing speed of travel to conserve energy does not appeal to them.

Do you think most people answer opinion poll questions honestly and accurately?
- Opinion polls probably reflect people's opinions when they answer the questions, though sometimes they may give the answer they think the questioner wants to hear.
- But if respondents saw some new information in a newspaper or on television, they could give very different answers within a few days.
- 'Deliberative polling' can show amazing switches in viewpoints if and when people are encouraged to focus on an issue in greater depth.

Margin questions

Have we heard so much about the dangers of global warming that we have started to lose interest?
More people are aware of the problem but many still do not understand how they can contribute to reducing greenhouse gas emissions. The campaign has started, but certainly not been completed, so continued pressure is needed. Sometimes people need to be persuaded with a 'carrot and stick' approach – paying more tax if you have a gas-guzzling car but being given a financial incentive to insulate your home or use renewable energy.

Review and research

How effective are international agreements on global warming?
Although the Kyoto Protocol was agreed in 1997, it did not take effect until 2005 when sufficient countries had signed up to it. Initially Russia, Canada, the USA, Australia, China and India did not back the plan. Canada and India signed in 2002, Russia in 2004 and Australia in 2007 – the change of president in the USA

has raised hopes that that country will adopt a much more positive attitude at the Copenhagen Summit in 2009. As 'developing countries', China and India are not required to reduce emissions at present but now that China emits more greenhouse gases than the USA, it is clear why it needs to be included in global efforts if climate change is to be resisted effectively.

How does the media present the activities of environmental groups?

- Often the media focuses attention on disruptive activities of environmental groups - Greenpeace disrupting Japanese efforts to kill whales or Plane Stupid's efforts to cause chaos at airports and disrupt travel.
- A danger with the environment issue is that people see the problem as too big for them to be able to make a difference.
- Citizenship reminds us that if we act individually or together we can make a difference - if we all make a little difference it can cause a bigger change in the end - and indeed in the case of the environment we have a moral duty to do so.

Is it ever right for environmental campaigners to break the law?

- Historically, campaigners from the suffragettes onwards have broken the law to highlight what they saw as a wrong - in their case - the refusal by men to allow them to vote.
- Such campaigns can have a bigger impact on public opinion than speeches or newspaper articles, however carefully reasoned.
- Those who break the law know they may be punished but feel the publicity gained and inconvenience caused by their activities will increase the chance of their goals being achieved.
- It is always wrong to break the law - but doing so out of moral conviction rather than personal gain may be less objectionable - but is still going to lead to punishment.
- Sometimes environmental campaigners such as the Kingsnorth Six find that a jury is in tune with their moral convictions and unwilling to convict them even though they did appear to be guilty.

CITIZENSHIP STUDIES

The UK economy: A question of tax

Lesson objectives	Specification link: Unit 1, Theme 3
By the end of this spread the student should: • know about different forms of local and national taxes, including income tax, VAT and council tax • understand why poorer people often pay a higher proportion of their income in tax than rich people • recognise the decisions local and national government have to make to provide services	

Focus

...on the difference between direct and indirect tax and the 'fairness' issue – why do people with lower incomes sometimes have to pay more tax than those with higher incomes?

Key terms

• government borrowing

• Budget

• direct taxes – e.g. income tax, council tax

• green taxes – e.g. congestion charge

• indirect taxes – e.g. VAT, fuel and alcohol taxes

• public services – e.g. NHS, police or education

Starter	Question: If a government needs to spend £1 million, where does it get the money from? Answer: taxes (direct and indirect), charges (e.g. prescription charges) or borrowing.
Development	How does income tax work? Use a simple example. If the personal allowance was £5,000 on which no tax was payable and the standard rate of tax was 20%, then a person earning £15,000 a year would pay 20% x £(15,000 – 5,000 = 10,000) = £2,000. If earnings over £40,000 attract a tax rate of 40%, someone earning £60,000 per year would pay:
	First £5,000 – nothing
	£5,001–£40,000 (20% tax) = £7,000
	£40,001–£60,000 (40% tax) = £8,000
	The person's total income tax bill would be £15,000. Low earners pay a lower proportion of income in income tax than higher earners (progressive principle), though higher earners can cut tax by making pension contributions or investing in new businesses.
	How does indirect tax work? Taxes such as VAT are charged on many goods we buy. Such purchases are the same for everyone, so low earners will pay a higher proportion of income on indirect taxes than high earners, who may be able to save more money. If government spending rises, will taxes have to go up? In the long run, yes. In the short term a government will close the gap between tax revenues received and spending by borrowing. In 2009/10, the Government expected to borrow £175,000,000,000 – it will have to pay interest on it and the whole sum must eventually be repaid.
Plenary	Go over the *Checklist* points. Students could work on the *Further issues* questions as research or homework. Or they can consider how and why income tax payers are allowed to reduce tax by claiming

allowances – e.g. for pension contributions.

Answers to questions in the Student Book

What's the issue?

Why has the government introduced some green taxes and what will the money be spent on?
- Government aims to charge people for activities that can damage the environment.
- They have created disincentives to driving vehicles, especially those with high carbon emissions.
- Income received from such taxes funds other moves to make the environment greener – reducing energy use through insulation or compensating for the removal of road fund taxes on low emissions vehicles.
- It has been suggested that, if taxes were used to discourage activities that harm the environment, the rate of income tax could be cut from 20p in £ to 16p in £.

What other reasons are there for introducing green taxes. How might these taxes affect you?
- Road pricing and more congestion charges are under discussion.
- Tax discs cost more for cars with high carbon emissions than for those with lower emissions.
- Above inflation increases on petrol and diesel tax aim to get more people to switch to public transport.

Why does the government have less money coming in from taxes and other sources than it expected?
In 2008 and 2009, company profits declined, some businesses collapsed, employment fell, unemployment rose, bank lending and credit card lending fell dramatically and consequently there was a big fall in company receipts and, therefore, tax payments. Individuals paid less income tax and, as shoppers became more reluctant to spend, income from indirect taxes such as VAT also declined.

What does the government spend the money on that it receives from taxes?
Government spending pays for public services such as the NHS and education. Although police forces, education, fire, personal social services, libraries, etc. are run by local councils, about half the funding comes from government grants that 'top up' councils' income from council tax (paid by individuals), business rates (paid by businesses) and charges (e.g. car parking charges).

Margin questions

Should taxation be switched more from direct to indirect taxes?
- If the government depended more on indirect taxes than direct taxes, taxation would take less account of people's income and ability to pay.
- This would break the progressive principle and be considered by many as unfair.

How important are green taxes?
See *Review and research* below.

Review and research

Should people on high salaries be taxed at a higher rate than lower earners?
- If everyone paid the same amount of tax – say £100 a week – this would be crippling to people earning only £200 a week but be hardly noticeable to someone earning £2,000 a week.
- So it seems fair that people with higher incomes should pay more. This could be achieved by saying that everyone would pay tax at 25% after account had been taken of their need for basic essentials such as housing and other costs (reflected in personal allowances).
- The argument for stepping up tax rates is one of fairness. From 2010, once someone is earning over £100,000, they will have an income tax rate of 50%. The argument for this is that it is fairer than charging 50% income tax on modest incomes which may be only 10% of this, around £10,000.
- People with higher incomes can afford to pay a higher proportion in tax.
- Those who oppose this policy see it as penalising enterprising people on whom the country's whole wealth partly depends.

CITIZENSHIP STUDIES

Is income tax a good way to share out wealth?

- To some extent the income tax system redistributes income by charging high earners a higher proportion of income in tax than those on more modest incomes.
- The income tax system also raises the income of very low income individuals by paying credits to them.
- Some people argue that minimum income levels should be higher for everyone, then it would be unnecessary to introduce complicated and costly schemes to raise incomes.
- Some people argue that if we were taxed less, we would spend more and stimulate the economy, creating new jobs and reducing unemployment benefits—a major area of government spending.

Are green taxes a way to change behaviour or are they just a way to raise extra revenue for the government?

- The idea behind green taxes is that we should tax people on things we want them to stop doing.
- But if such taxes were totally successful, people would stop doing these activities and then government would derive little or no income from them.
- Many people would be more willing to accept green taxes if they were spent on supporting the environment or, alternatively, if other taxes were reduced by a corresponding amount every time a green tax was raised.

CITIZENSHIP STUDIES

Benefits and spending

Lesson objectives	Specification link: Unit 1, Theme 3
By the end of this spread the student should: • understand the means test debate • recognise the boundary between public and private sectors • be aware of priorities and choices when allocating spending between education, health, welfare and transport	

Focus

...on arguments for and against public and private provision – and the choices involved.

Key terms

- choices
- means test
- poverty
- priorities

- Private Finance Initiatives
- Public Private Partnerships
- shareholders
- welfare state

Starter	Focus on the 'Breadline Britain' quote. Why would people not apply for benefits to which they were entitled? Answers should be (i) don't know or understand the system or (ii) don't wish to give away their private details or (iii) don't want to be a 'charity case'.
Development	**Do means tests do more harm than good?** They allow government to focus scarce funds on those who most need support. But the price of this is that many people never claim. Others say that if savings mean you don't get support, it may be better not to save for the future.
	Are services better run by the Government or private companies? Margaret Thatcher's Government privatised many former state-run industries such as gas, electricity, telephones and airports, thereby turning many UK citizens into shareholders. Privatising the railways did not work well and was greatly changed by Tony Blair's Government.
	What are the strengths and weaknesses of PFI and PPP arrangements? If the private sector can organise projects more efficiently than the public sector, it is a good idea to get a private company/group of companies to build a new school or hospital and then get the school or hospital to run the service and spread the cost over 25 or 30 years. Critics say this means too much public money is paid over as profits or interest to the PPPs; they challenge the idea that it would be impossible for the public sector to create such new schools or hospitals themselves.
	Making choices: should we be building railway lines rather than new roads or airport runways? Such questions involve economic, social and political choices – motorists want roads, environmentalists would probably favour railways and reject more airport runways.

Plenary	Go over the *Checklist* points. Students can work on the *Further issues* questions as research or homework e.g. they could consider why the Millennium Dome was seen as a failure but is now a success as the O2 Arena.

Answers to questions in the Student Book

What's the issue?

Who is at fault when people do not apply for the benefits they are entitled to?
- The Benefits Agency is required to publicise people's entitlements to benefits.
- Welfare organisations (Citizens Advice Bureau, Help the Aged and Age Concern) also publicise entitlements.
- But many people, particularly the elderly, dislike the idea of 'charity', find the application process confusing and are often reluctant to discuss their private affairs with others.
- If Government sets up a system in which people are reluctant to participate, can anyone be at fault but the Government itself?

Should tax be increased to give more money to pensioners so that they do not live in poverty?
- The argument against means tested benefits is that they miss out some people who need financial help if they do not apply because they dislike the procedure.
- The alternative would be to have a 'universal benefit' paid to everyone automatically.
- This would add to government spending but would probably be less cumbersome, complicated (and therefore expensive) than present means tested benefits.
- Some increases in taxation might be needed if the system was changed but, overall, the change in expenditure could be modest.

Is it more important for local authorities to provide services for the elderly than for young people?
- Everyone has rights – the young as much as older people need support from personal social services and education.
- So choosing between one group and another – young or old – is difficult to justify.
- Councils with limited budgets have to ration spending because they can only stretch budgets to go so far.
- Thus they have difficult choices to make unless there is enough finance available to meet all proven needs.

Margin questions

Should everyone be entitled to the same welfare cover or should state resources be targeted at those with the greatest needs? What is a 'minimum safety net'?
A minimum safety net provides people with basic accommodation and enough money to feed themselves and other family members. Most people believe the standards guaranteed by the welfare state should be above this 'poverty level'. Targeting saves governments and councils money but, if some people don't apply, they miss out altogether. Some universal benefits such as child benefit are taxable so low income people pay little or no tax on them while high earners have to repay 40% of the benefit in tax.

What are the advantages and disadvantages of using PFI and PPP?
See *Development* section on previous page.

Should we build more railways and trams rather than more roads?
Rail travel is far less damaging to the environment than road travel. There seems to be growing support for more train and tram systems, new railway lines and better rolling stock to enable more people to travel reliably and safely by such systems. Birmingham/Wolverhampton, Sheffield, Nottingham, Tyne & Wear, Croydon and Manchester are areas where new tram systems have greatly reduced road congestion.

Will a new runway at Heathrow Airport be an expensive environmental disaster?
Flights are far more damaging to the environment than road or rail journeys. According to Lord Turner, Chair of the Committee on Climate Change, ideally, technologies need to be developed for aircraft to use biofuels. If this cannot be achieved, the demand for air travel will need to be curtailed through high charges and the provision of speedy, cost-effective alternatives such as high-speed rail.

Are private toll motorways the best way to improve the road system?
The M6 Private Toll Motorway (Birmingham Northern Relief Road) which opened in December 2003 is much less congested than the publicly-funded M6. If there were charges to use both roads, the balance of usage could be very different. The existence of two roads going in the same directions has resulted in reduced journey times for most motorists.

Review and research

Should the government encourage people to use private health insurance so that more of the National Health budget can be used to help the really needy?
Encouraging some people to get health insurance while others depend on the NHS could lead to accusations of two-tier health provision. The Beveridge report in 1942, which led to the formation of the welfare state, recommended a 'cradle to grave' service for all in the country. NHS costs have risen as new drug therapies have been developed to which all people need access if they experience particular health problems. Suggestions that poorer people might use the NHS while others use private medicine would undermine the NHS philosophy of caring for all. But if some people prefer to use private medicine as a matter of personal choice, they should be free to do so.

Are state welfare costs too high and should they be reduced?
- All governments are looking for better cost-effectiveness.
- Heathcare and personal care costs are high, not least as a result of expensive drugs being developed.
- The National Institute of Health and Clinical Excellence (NICE) aims to ensure that new drugs are used only if they contribute significantly to overcoming illness and improving health.
- One way to reduce costs would be to increase charges on some users or some treatments.
- This could create a two-tier service, which many people would find unacceptable.

How should governments decide welfare spending priorities?
Governments need to be certain about the problems to be addressed and to be flexible in finding effective solutions. A person of right wing and Conservative views would believe less should be spent and more individuals should take responsibility for their own care, through health insurance if necessary. A person with social democratic instincts would believe that all should enjoy an equally high standard and that to tell poor people they must take responsibility for their own social welfare is unrealistic, an absurdity and a fiction. 'Rationing' welfare spending leads to delays in treatment and lengthy waiting lists.

Managing the economy

Lesson objectives	Specification link: Unit 1, Theme 3
By the end of this spread the student should: • understand how the government aims to reduce unemployment • recognise why the government has introduced a points-based immigration scheme for economic migrants with scarce skills • know about the effect on the economy of the UK's ageing population and increased life expectancy	

Focus

...on the linkages between birth rate, ageing population, life expectancy, retirement ages and migration.

Key terms

• ageing population

• discrimination

• full employment and unemployment

• life expectancy

• migration and economic migrants

• points-based immigration

Linked activity sheets

• How the economy functions

Starter	Start with the comings and goings. Why do 400,000 people from this country go to live in other parts of the world every year? They want to work or retire to EU countries, Australia, New Zealand or the USA. Why do 600,000 come to live in this country every year? Distinguish carefully between asylum seekers and economic migrants. Note that people from EU countries can come to live and work in the UK as people from the UK can go to live or work in other EU countries.
Development	Focus on key features of the labour market in recent years: • Declining birth rate • Young workers stay in education longer (few prospects for young unskilled workers) • More female workers • Dependence on many workers from overseas to fill skills shortages. • Introduction of a points-based immigration scheme • Older workers reaching retirement age (with plans to raise retirement age). The proportion of workers generating national income that must partly support the population as a whole is at a record low, creating a heavy burden for all workers. The 2008/9 credit crunch led to the recent recession with many businesses failing and millions of workers losing their jobs. Government acted to minimise job losses and business failures and to stimulate growth as part of its duty to manage the economy.

Plenary	Revise the *Checklist* points. Students can work on the *Further issues* questions as research or homework. Or they could think about whether asylum seekers should be allowed to work in the UK (when the UK is short of workers and at or near full employment) or be paid benefits if they cannot get work.

Answers to questions in the Student Book

What's the issue?

Can the UK benefit from high levels of economic migration (when people move from one country to another in search of employment or for other economic reasons)?

- Increasingly Europe's 'single market' for trading is becoming a 'single market' for labour.
- Many UK workers go to work in other EU countries just as EU citizens come to work in the UK.
- Many companies in all countries are multinationals with production and trading operations in many different countries – and staff moving between them.
- In view of the declining birth rate and the ageing population, the UK has benefited from the willingness of many skilled workers from overseas to come to occupy unfilled job vacancies.

What are the implications for the economy of rising numbers of healthy elderly people?

- Increasing numbers of elderly people will place a heavy burden on the UK economy in terms of their pension entitlements.
- Schemes have been introduced to allow them to continue working into retirement and to defer pensions until later (in return for an additional bonus).
- In future years, the retirement age will rise to 68 years for both men and women.
- A larger, older population will have big implications for the NHS as people live longer.
- Life expectancy is rising as people live healthier lifestyles but, as activity ratios fall, the working population faces a big burden in paying the taxes to finance government programmes.

Should we be more concerned by high levels of migration than by an increasingly elderly population?

- Many economic migrants from other countries generate much income and wealth in the country, pay substantial taxes and employ substantial numbers of people – their presence is undoubtedly an advantage to the economy.
- Britain has traditionally welcomed asylum seekers – people fleeing from persecution in other parts of the world – but at present such workers are not allowed to take employment.
- Some people might question whether this rule should continue, particularly when the UK is at or near full employment and is short of workers with specific skills.
- In the short term, even if retirement ages are marginally changed, the only ways to increase the number of workers to fill job vacancies are either to get more people such as single mothers to enter the labour market or else to attract workers to fill skill shortage areas.
- The points-based immigration scheme is designed to ensure that more non-EU workers do not come from overseas when there is a shortage of jobs in the UK.

How is the UK's ageing population and increased life expectancy affecting our economy?

- As an average, a baby born in 2009 is likely to live to about 80 years.
- This figure has increased substantially over recent years, as welfare benefits have been widely shared and as housing, health, education and income standards have risen.
- Raising the compulsory schooling to 18 means that the UK is planning to have a better educated/trained workforce with the skill to exploit new technologies and achieve greater productivity.
- The higher the proportion of elderly (non-working) people in the population, the greater the burden on those at work in terms of the amount of tax they need to pay to fund pensions, NHS, personal care, etc. of the elderly as well as paying for education for the young.

Margin questions

If pensions become inadequate, do you think some people might decide not to retire at all?
Some people enjoy working and recent age discrimination legislation is giving them a better chance of continuing in employment until later in life. Most people are likely to retire at some stage but as many private pension schemes have failed to generate pension levels initially hoped for, there are likely to be some elderly workers who seek to stay in employment as long as they are physically able.

Should the government try to reduce the need for skilled migrant workers? What could it do?
- Government policies to raise the school leaving age and training to 18 mean we have a better chance of creating a skilled workforce; all young workers should get an improved chance to achieve their potential.
- Taking skilled migrant workers from other countries may help Britain but may deprive their own country of the benefits it could gain from their work. This is particularly true of doctors and health workers.
- It would be a mistake to think that work in the UK can only be done by UK workers.
- Globalisation throughout the economy means it is increasingly likely that more and more people from all over the world will spend some of their working life in employment in different countries.

Review and research

Why is the age structure of the population changing?
Essentially the birth rate has fallen – more people live single lives, fewer people are getting married and more cohabiting, civil partnerships between same-sex couples are now increasingly accepted socially, divorce remains high, the elderly are living much longer as rates of life expectancy increase and the average size of households has dropped significantly. The reasons for such changes undoubtedly include factors such as:
- More people get degrees and can lead successful independent lives.
- More women now focus on their careers before thinking of getting married or having children.
- Costs of marriages have increased sharply causing many people to decide to cohabit rather than marry.
- Illegitimacy of children is now less likely to be frowned upon.
- Whereas unhappy couples used to stay married 'for the sake of the children' it is increasingly recognised that being brought up in an unhappy home is good neither for children nor parents.
- Gay or lesbian lifestyles is now widely accepted.
- Life expectancy has increased thanks to improved health and welfare.

How can the government increase the proportion of the working-age population?
- Attract economic migrants to the country.
- Allow asylum seekers in the country to take paid employment.
- Encourage single mothers and others not seeking employment to look for jobs and to accept training to be able to do them.
- Enable those with disabilities or long-term illness to obtain employment and training.
- Raise the retirement age.
- Try to abolish the concept of retirement altogether.

Should people have greater responsibility to provide for their retirement?
- A person who will have to live on the state pension only is likely to have an impoverished old age.
- Over the past 30 or more years people have been encouraged to invest in pensions and been given generous tax breaks to do so – yet these pensions have often yielded disappointing returns – and when the Equitable Life Assurance Society almost failed, pensioners lost much of their pension savings.
- This has made people wary of private pension schemes – not least because the Government has been reluctant to compensate those who lost out because of Equitable Life even though they happily guaranteed the savings of those whose money had been deposited in banks that proved to be insolvent.
- Many people now see their homes as an important form of saving for retirement – yet the drop in values during the credit crunch highlighted the weakness of such a strategy.
- As long as Government insists on means-testing pension credit (for low income pensioners), those who try to save or provide for themselves are effectively penalising themselves by taking themselves above the thresholds that could trigger top-up payments, thereby providing a big disincentive for saving.

CITIZENSHIP STUDIES

Communities in the UK:
Individuals making a difference

Lesson objectives	Specification link: Unit 1, Theme 3
By the end of this spread the student should: • know how individuals can make a difference to community life • understand how individuals working together in groups can raise funds for causes they support • recognise how individuals contribute to community cohesion	

Focus

...on how and why individuals can try to change things (whether it is doing great work and setting a positive example like Jane Tomlinson and Richard Harvey) or gaining sponsorship to support a local or national charity by running a marathon to help the local hospice or air ambulance – or to help local children keep healthy by coaching sports or to support the elderly or disabled people by delivering meals to them.

Key terms

- charities e.g. Mencap, RNIB, Wilts Air Ambulance
- community and community cohesion
- sponsorship
- voluntary work

Starter	Start with the community. What is a community? It is a group of people with shared interests and loyalties.
Development	It may be the residents of a particular estate or village or suburb. But it may also involve people with a common ethnicity – we often speak of, for example, the Chinese community. Communities may also involve people with shared professional interests – accountants, lawyers, doctors. Why are such networks so important? Then ask students to think about why people do things without pay. Maybe they want to raise funds to find cures for strokes, or cancer or heart disease. Maybe they have a natural human desire to help people they know and like. If you have time, find out more from the Internet about both Jane Tomlinson and Richard Harvey. Ask the students to think about people nationally or locally who have raised money for worthwhile causes – e.g. Ian Botham or Ranulph Fiennes at a national level. Research websites of a few national charities – help the students to understand how such charities make a difference Can the students think of people who do voluntary work locally as a good citizen? (Perhaps the students could interview some of them or maybe they could come and tell students about the work they do.)
Plenary	Go over the *Checklist* points. Students could work on the *Further issues* questions as research or homework. Or they could research national charities – the money they raise, what happens as a result of their efforts, what would NOT happen without their efforts.

Answers to questions in the Student Book

What's the issue?

Why do so many people work hard for no pay or reward?
- Often people work hard to support and maintain their local church.
- Sometimes they do so out of moral or religious conviction, not 'walking by on the other side' and ignoring the needs of those less fortunate than ourselves.
- Sometimes people do voluntary work linked to the interests of members of their own friends and family – coaching children or others in particular sports, helping a local hospice, raising more funds for the school their children attend (or perhaps they attended in the past).
- The schools and hospitals in many towns were originally established with cash raised by voluntary work and individual subscriptions – now such organisations are part of the local education authority or the local NHS but people still feel they want to support them financially.
- Giving time and money to a charity is an unselfish act (look at the excellent work done by air ambulances funded by charity in many parts of the UK) and we see immediately the positive results that follow.
- No wonder local people who help out feel proud of such achievements.

How important is voluntary work to community cohesion?
- Talking part in voluntary activities shows you share the same goals as others who take part.
- It sets up a sense of 'togetherness' with everyone looking out for each other.
- Even if people don't agree on every issue, they know they are all on the same side.
- Community spirit binding people together, or 'cohesion', was seen in mining communities when pit closures were proposed.
- A similar spirit could be seen in 2007 on the remote Shetland Islands when over half the islanders joined a successful campaign to save a young Thai man, Sakchai Makao, from being deported. Sakchai had lived on the islands since he was 10 years old – a case of 'all of us for one of us'.
- Networks of local people who support the church and other organisations get involved in everything from local charity flag days to campaigning to keep the local school or post office open if it is under threat.
- Such activities are often seen as the lifeblood of a community where people look out for and help each other.

Is it better for social change to be brought about by voluntary work and charities or by government?
- A government or council programme often involves paying people to do particular jobs.
- No matter how good the employees are, they are not likely to be as interested, involved or enthusiastic as local people who see a particular local charity or project as 'theirs'.
- Local people working together to achieve something for their local community are likely to persist till they have won through and then make sure that the project thrives and succeeds.

Margin questions

What would happen if people gave up doing voluntary work? What would happen if many more people did charity work?
- No flag days, no summer fetes trying to raise funds for good causes, no individuals giving up hours of their time to coach local youngsters in swimming, football, orienteering, boxing etc.
- In fact, no one doing anything for anyone else – a very selfish, inward-looking materialistic society.
- The more people supporting local charities, the more likely good causes are to succeed.
- One of the developments that has given a boost to charities and good causes is the National Lottery, which has provided funding to get many worthwhile schemes off the ground.
- Look at the National Lottery website to find out how much has been given to causes. In June 2009 the figure was £22 billion.

CITIZENSHIP STUDIES

Review and research

Should hospitals depend on voluntary efforts to provide essential equipment such as an air ambulance?

Communities take pride in what they achieve for themselves and for each other. In Wiltshire, as a result of volunteers raising £320,000 a year for the local air ambulance, hundreds of people have been airlifted to hospitals for urgent medical treatment – in some cases saving their lives. People feel good about playing their part in raising cash for such a good cause. If hospitals and schools did not allow individuals and groups to work together to help provide improvements in local services, the services would probably be the poorer and local people would have their sense of 'get-up-and-go' or 'empowerment' taken away from them.

Why do strong voluntary and charitable networks seem to add to the self-confidence and cohesion of an area?

- When people working together voluntarily for their community and no personal reward actually achieve their goals, this sets up a sense of pride and achievement.
- Once it has been proved that the community can achieve things, more people are likely to get involved and community agendas often become more ambitious.

Should all young people be expected to do national service in the community - locally, nationally or globally - for two years after leaving school, college or university?

- Increasing numbers of young people spend time helping people in overseas countries in a gap year between school and university.
- The idea that more young people should find ways to help individuals and communities in the UK itself has been widely discussed over the years.
- President Obama has made a similar proposal in the USA.
- Whether it is reasonable to say 'all must' is open to debate but many young people say they would welcome the opportunity to help people in need or to make a difference in their own community.

Working together

Lesson objectives	Specification link: Unit 1, Theme 3
By the end of this spread the student should: • understand how and why communities change over time and the role of the voluntary sector in supporting them at local, national and global level • know about the impact of business on employment opportunities and community spending • recognise government's role in ensuring that businesses flourish and citizens prosper in a free and fair economy	

Focus

...on the idea of changes in communities – are there parts of your area where a new estate has been built or an area that used to be a separate village is now a suburb in a larger town? What are the links between businesses, employment and transport to dictate how communities change? Why are inner cities so different from suburbs? Why is urban life so different from living in the countryside?

Key terms

• building societies and credit unions

• commuting and car-sharing

• free and fair trade

• public transport – bus, tram and train

• second homes

• social housing

Linked activity sheets

• Fair trade

• The decline of rural communities

Starter	Working together involves co-operating. This could be building societies or credit unions where members form a society to save money or get a mortgage. Ask students: in what other ways do people work together co-operatively to make things happen?
Development	Many people in rural areas where public transport is poor or non-existent engage in car-sharing. Often farmers set up a co-operative to produce food together. The Co-op societies throughout Britain raise the profile of and promote fair trade. (Make sure students understand the difference between free trade and fair trade.)
	Let students explore why some people believe the countryside is in decline. Emphasise: second homes push up house prices, social housing for rent is in short supply so young people brought up in the countryside are forced out of the villages into the towns, so their children go to town schools rather than village schools and the village schools are being closed down. Why is public transport so poor in rural areas? – sparse population and many people have cars. Why are 65% of people who live in the country of pension age, but only 15% in urban areas? – many people retire to the countryside; many born in the countryside move away to get work and housing.
	While most people who lived in the countryside used to work in farming or related trades, many now live in the countryside and either commute to towns to work or spend much working time at

	home communicating via broadband.
	Get the students to think about the biggest difference between living in a rural area or a town or city.
Plenary	Go over the *Checklist* points. Students could work on the *Further issues* questions as research or homework. Or you may want them to find out about how fair trade supports local Agenda 21.

Answers to questions in the Student Book

What's the issue?

Why have rural communities declined in recent years?
- Farming employs many fewer people.
- Many rural railway stations have closed and buses run only infrequently.
- As more people shop in town supermarkets, village shops and post offices get insufficient custom to continue.
- Often people buy second homes in the countryside for occasional use, pushing up the price of housing beyond anything young people brought up in the countryside can afford.
- So the young people move to the town to get a home or jobs or both and therefore their children go to town schools rather than village schools – so the village school often closes.

How do you account for the biggest differences between rural and urban communities?
- There is a massive age gap – 15% are over 65 in towns, 65% in the countryside.
- There are ten times more non-white people in country areas than in the towns.
- Twice as many people in the countryside work at home than in the towns.
- The rate of self-employment in country areas is almost twice that in urban areas.
- About 10% more workers in rural areas travel to work by car or van than those living in towns.
- Commuting to work distances average seven miles in urban areas but 11 miles in rural areas.

What steps could be taken to restore rural communities?
- Social housing could be built to enable young people to rent a home in their village or a nearby one.
- Their children could then go to a local village school.
- With all political parties recognising the need for more housing, this could be built in areas where more people would justify keeping/re-opening a school, village store or post office.
- With many businesses communicating with their customers by broadband, which has now been installed in many rural areas, many jobs in towns could easily be relocated to small country towns or villages to provide employment opportunities for firms – or more people may choose to become self-employed.
- If more people lived in particular villages, railway stations could be opened or re-opened in areas where lines still exist, or better bus services provided.
- Since the arrival of second-home owners has contributed to social breakdown, should such people be made to pay much higher taxes – e.g. triple council tax?
- A vibrant countryside can provide tourist opportunities and many opportunities for leisure activities and catering.

Margin questions

Would it be a good idea to re-open any rural railway stations that have been closed or would it just be a waste of money?
- A vibrant countryside can provide tourist opportunities and many opportunities for leisure activities and catering.
- New tram systems often built on old railway lines have proved to be an enormous success.
- In some areas where railway lines still operate, the numbers of potential commuters have risen sharply in the 40 years since the Beeching cuts when many stations closed. There is a case for re-opening some, but probably not all.
- One of the stations closed in the 1960s that re-opened recently is Laurencekirk in Aberdeenshire; its opening was said to open up the whole area for jobs, commuting and leisure.

- Some of the proposed new eco-towns will need linking to the national rail infrastructure - e.g. the proposed Middle Quinton could easily justify a rail link to Stratford-on-Avon and/or Honeybourne on the Worcester-London main line.

What arguments could be put forward to support re-opening them? How might a new station support the local community?

- A railway station provides easy access to workplaces miles away and new homes built in a village may be less expensive than those built in the towns themselves.
- A boost in a village population can change the age profile and increase support for sports clubs, country pursuits (shooting, orienteering, etc.), pubs, restaurants, local businesses including post offices and schools.
- If fewer people use cars and more people use rail, the resulting carbon emissions are greatly reduced.

Review and research

How could incomes and business activity in rural areas be increased so that village shops, schools, pubs and post offices could be re-opened?

See 'What steps could be taken to restore rural communities?' above.

When is it best to provide a service for the community through a partnership rather than through the government alone?

Partnerships of local firms, societies or organisations (e.g. crime partnerships or business partnerships) provide networks through which people and firms can communicate, share and discuss problems or difficulties and work together to find solutions. The more people, firms or organisations are involved the greater the chance a particular project will succeed because, once people feel a commitment to a project, they won't want to let other people down. Such loyalty and commitment is rarely evident in a project devised and launched by government alone.

Do goods imported as a result of free trade or fair trade help or hinder the prospects of UK producers and supermarkets?

- Fair trade - providing a market for goods produced co-operatively by people in less economically developed countries - is enthusiastically promoted by the Co-op and other supermarket chains in the UK.
- Goods produced by fair trade groups include coffee, tea, bananas and other produce from tropical areas that are no competition for UK producers.
- Since UK people have embraced the ideas of free and fair trade enthusiastically, UK supermarkets recognise that offering fair trade goods in their stores is welcomed by customers.
- The more customers go to their stores, the more items will be sold - including those produced in the UK by UK producers - so everyone is a winner.

CITIZENSHIP STUDIES

The UK's role in the world: An ethical foreign policy

Lesson objectives	Specification link: Unit 1, Theme 3
By the end of this spread the student should: • understand how ethics can affect policy making and policy goals • recognise the nature and impact of UK global diplomacy • understand key features of a morally justifiable view of trade	

Focus

...on the difference between ethical and unethical foreign policies. An ethical foreign policy involves giving humanitarian aid, combating climate change, resisting discrimination, opposing repressive regimes and intervening militarily to combat injustice.

Key terms

- balance of trade
- corruption
- democracy
- ethical or unethical
- free and fair trade
- genocide
- imports and exports
- international trade
- peacekeeping
- World Trade Organization

Starter	What might an unethical foreign policy involve? Get students to think of some examples.
Development	Perhaps: • ignoring human rights • not being open and honest about our aims or objectives • torturing suspects or practising genocide • corruptly going to war to steal another country's land or resources such as oil or gold • ruining producers in developing countries by flooding their markets with cheap subsidised goods. When countries disagree, the best way to find agreement is to meet and negotiate. Eventually one country will persuade the other, often with compromises on both sides and 'give-and-take' between them. By contrast, an ethical policy means being open and honest, sticking to one's promises and helping other friends of the UK such as Israel and the Palestine territories to sort out their differences. Through its membership of the Commonwealth, the European Union and the United Nations, the UK aims to promote international trade (in particular, free and fair trade) as well as offering humanitarian aid at times of civil unrest, massive flooding, earthquakes, etc.
Plenary	Go over the *Checklist* points. Students can work on the *Further issues* questions as research or homework or you may want them to find out about fair trade products on sale in local shops.

Answers to questions in the Student Book

What's the issue?

How has the government tried to support 'democratic rights' in other countries?
- Many Commonwealth countries based their own systems of government on the UK model – and some elements remain even when changes have subsequently been introduced.
- It is ironic that, as a result of the influence of the UK, many countries now elect parliaments through proportional representation, something that doesn't actually happen in the UK for elections to the Westminster Parliament.
- When Commonwealth countries abandon democracy or deny human rights, they may be suspended from the Commonwealth – e.g. South Africa, Pakistan and Zimbabwe – often returning later when democracy has been fully re-established.
- When defeated countries were reconstructed after World War 2 they were rebuilt as democracies.
- Like other democratic countries, the UK often sends observers to monitor elections abroad and reports are often issued commenting on the progress being made in newly democratic countries such as Russia and Indonesia.
- The British Council has premises all over the world to spread understanding and awareness of UK values and ways of doing things – just as the BBC also adds to knowledge about Britain through its World Service.

Should Britain send troops or economic aid to places where people are suffering and starving as the result of corrupt government or civil war?
- If people are starving or in great distress, there is a natural desire to help them – that is what drives the humanitarian motives of government, charities and the whole population in the UK.
- Critics sometimes point out that much aid intended for the hungry is diverted, perhaps by a dictator's army.
- Or sometimes a corrupt government may try to sell to the country's poor the aid that other countries have freely given.
- Where people are in great distress, like the people of Zimbabwe, Darfur or Myanmar (Burma) in recent years, it has to be better to try to help than to do nothing at all.
- Sending troops to fight or engage in peacekeeping in another country needs to be clearly authorised by the United Nations – otherwise the independence or sovereignty of the country being 'invaded' will be compromised.
- If the UN feels forces need to be sent to various trouble spots (e.g. Sierra Leone, Afghanistan, former Yugoslavia), it would be unethical to leave the burden of providing troops to others – the UK needs to play its part just like other countries.

Why should Britain's foreign policy be ethical?
Many countries were quick to criticise the UK and USA for going to war with Iraq. It was said the two countries and their allies had their eyes on the oil reserves in Iraq. To go to war to steal a country's resources or to commit genocide to gain territory is wholly out of place in the twenty-first century. If the UK wants to be an honest broker in a peaceful world, respected and believed, it must not behave in ways for which it can be criticised. Ethics involve behaving proportionately – for example, did Israel behave ethically or unethically in the 2009 conflict, when it killed at least 1,200 Palestinians, including many children and civilians, in Gaza Strip even though only 13 Israeli lives were lost?

Margin questions

Does the British government always follow an ethical foreign policy?
If the UK is proved to have known about or participated in extraordinary rendition (rendering terrorist suspects to third countries where torture is acceptable), then it would be difficult to show that its foreign policy was truly ethical. If we 'dump' our food surpluses at very low prices into markets in developing countries, ruining local producers in so doing, then our policies are not ethical. If in the nineteenth and twentieth centuries, the UK colonised some countries and exploited their resources for our own gain, that also would not have been ethical. But in modern times our policies for promoting democracy, climate change, international development, world trade, human rights and peacekeeping have set a good example to the rest of the world.

CITIZENSHIP STU

What different factors can influence foreign policy?

Foreign policy can be influenced by social, economic and political factors. All countries want to maximise their rights to scarce resources (as the UK did when we developed oil and gas fields in the North Sea) and there is a similar international chess game going on as world powers position themselves to gain many of the resources thought to exist in the Arctic and Antarctic regions. Often issues are resolved by international diplomacy – through its stance in the Commonwealth, the European Union and the United Nations, the UK seeks to develop coalitions and alliances so that it can influence outcomes and events about which it is concerned – the more countries willing to vote with the UK in international forums, the greater its chance of being influential. Although it is more pleasant to be friends with another country than to be sharply critical, there are times when an honest country will feel it has to express its opposition as the UK has over the murderous Mugabe regime in Zimbabwe, Chinese repression in Tibet or the brutality of the undemocratic generals in Myanmar (Burma).

Review and research

Should foreign policy be based on ethical principles rather than UK self-interest?

No one should expect the UK to act against its own self-interest any more than any other country. But in seeking to build up our share of world trade or to promote reductions in carbon emissions, we should be open and honest, stick to our word, not let people down or take advantage of them or their countries.

What are the benefits to the UK of a free trade policy?

A big help to businesses in the UK is that the country is part of the EU Single Market. Over the 27 member countries there are no tariffs and goods, services and workers from one member state can move freely to and from other member states. This means there is a market with 500 million customers to which UK businesses can seek to export their goods. Of course firms in other countries can compete with our producers and the greatest success goes to those firms that can produce competitively and efficiently – to the benefit of consumers throughout the EU. The World Trade Organization has been trying to reduce tariffs to get nearer to achieving a world without such barriers to trade – but progress has been slow because the economic interests of developed and developing countries often differ.

The government claims to believe in fair trade. What obstacles do they face when trying to encourage fair trade with developing countries?

Normally multinational companies (Microsoft, Coca-Cola, BP, Prudential, Nike, HSBC) locate themselves where they can operate most cheaply and sell their goods for the greatest profits. Such companies are interested in profits rather than the welfare of citizens or producers in developing countries – this is a very different model from that offered by fair trade, where the focus is on paying a fair price to producers for their tea, coffee, bananas, textiles and so on, to raise their living standards and to allow them to share in the benefits of the trade in which they engage rather than being bullied into accepting unreasonably low prices.

CITIZENSHIP STUDIES

Britain and the European Union

Lesson objectives	Specification link: Unit 1, Theme 3
By the end of this spread the student should: • know about the aims, activities and membership of the EU • recognise the institutions that do the work of the EU • be aware of debates about the effectiveness of UK membership of the EU	

Focus

...on why the Common Market was established with six member countries in the 1950s and how it has developed into 27 countries in the 2000s with more countries wanting to join. If new countries are keen to join, why would the UK want to leave the EU?

Key terms

• bureaucracy

• Common Market

• Eurosceptics

• EU Parliament, Council or Minister, Commission and Court of Justice and Presidency

• Soviet bloc

Linked activity sheets

• UK relations with Europe – quiz

• The Commonwealth of Nations and the European Union

Starter	Why was the Common Market formed between France, Germany, Brussels, Luxembourg, Italy and Holland in the 1950s?
Development	The Common Market was formed so countries destroyed by war could rebuild physically and economically and to bind European nations so tightly together that there would be no more World Wars starting in Europe. This aim has been achieved, which is a remarkable achievement considering countries such as Poland, Slovakia, Slovenia, Lithuania and Estonia were previously part of the Soviet bloc of Communist countries.
	The goal of generating economic growth has been realised, though getting 27 different economies to converge when they started off with different levels of economic activity is still proving difficult.
	Countries joining since the Common Market was first formed – including the UK and Eire in 1972 – and those joining later, all recognise that many economic, social and political issues can be better addressed collectively than separately. This may be why Iceland's new PM sees EU membership as the answer to the country's economic problems.
	Global warming will only be tackled effectively by international agreement. The EU is well placed to be a big player in this area.
	EU countries working together over trade have the economic muscle to ensure they are not bullied by the USA.
	When a country is hit by a crisis, the EU helps them meet costs and to plan to put things right (UK after the 2007 floods and BSE crisis).

CITIZENSHIP STUDIES

Plenary	Go over the *Checklist* points. Students can work on the *Further issues* questions as research or homework. Or they could find out about the different policies of the main UK parties on European matters.

Answers to questions in the Student Book

What's the issue?

In what ways is the EU democratic and how is it bureaucratic?
- Over the years the EU has increased the powers of the European Parliament. MEPs are directly elected by PR from each of the 27 EU countries.
- The Parliament has greater powers to comment and vote on legislation proposed by the Commission. The Budget requires its approval before it can take effect.
- The Parliament also has the power to reject the Commission.
- Decisions taken in the Council of Ministers involve relevant ministers from each country (e.g. Agriculture minister for agriculture issues) who are democratically elected members by their own country's government.
- Bureaucracy (form of organisation that may be slow to respond and inflexible) exists in most large organisations, and there are further complications in an organisation where 23 languages are spoken.
- The Lisbon treaty is intended to reduce the bureaucracy and make the EU work better – now there are 27 members.
- Those who see the EU as 'undemocratic' complain that too many powers are transferred from individual countries to Europe. This is inevitable if global problems such as climate change or economic stability are now too big to be dealt with at national level.
- By having some decisions taken by EU bodies, individual countries have influence over what happens in the other member countries.

Is the EU too big and diverse to be effective internationally?
In trade negotiations, the collective power of the EU is much greater than that of individual countries. It would be easier to run the EU if countries had more in common and spoke the same language, yet the differences are a positive strength in accounting for the success of the Single Market, with different countries buying and selling different products to other member countries. The higher the number of members, the greater the potential progress in ensuring more countries commit to major projects, e.g. to tackle international crime or reverse global warming. For services that do not call for such cross-country co-ordination the most effective form of delivery is at national, regional or local level.

Which major political party is the most enthusiastic supporter of EU membership and which is the least enthusiastic?
At the time of the 2009 European Parliament elections, the Liberal Democrats, Labour and Greens were most positive about the EU, though with serious reservations on some issues, while Conservatives and UKIP were most critical (UKIP wishing to leave the EU altogether just as others are wanting to join).

Margin questions

Which European countries have currently applied to join the EU? Which European countries have chosen not to join? Why have they rejected membership?
Iceland, Republic of Macedonia, Croatia and perhaps Turkey are the most likely countries to join the EU with Ukraine and Georgia also possible future members. Norway and Switzerland have declined to join – Norway probably because it feared it would lose control of its fishing waters and Switzerland because it is keen to retain its long-standing position on unaligned neutrality.

What other institutions contribute to the work of the EU
The most important is the European Court of Justice, which deals with cases covering breaches of EU law. The European Court of Auditors checks expenditures to prevent or identify financial irregularities.

CITIZENSHIP STUDIES

Does it matter that the Parliament is the only democratically appointed EU institution?
The Parliament is gradually becoming more assertive and gaining more power. Members of other EU institutions also have acute democratic instincts. The Council of Ministers is made up of members of the governments (democratically elected) of each of the 27 member countries. Commission members are each nominated by one of the member governments and usually have good experience of working in a democratic organisation (e.g. recent Commissioner from the UK, Neil Kinnock, former Leader of the Labour Party). In 2009 the President of the European Commission was José Manuel Barroso, former Prime Minister of Portugal.

Review and research

Is the EU too large? Should countries outside Europe be allowed to join the EU?
- 'Too large' can really only be judged in the context of particular objectives. If global objectives are taken seriously, there can never be too much co-operation.
- But decision making and monitoring structures need to be amended and streamlined along the lines proposed by the Lisbon treaty or by other means.
- The focus of the organisation might become distracted if countries from other parts of the world joined.

What criteria should the EU expect new members to meet?
The so-called Copenhagen criteria were agreed as long ago as 1993. They say:
- To be accepted as a member, a country must have a good human rights record and be able to show it protects minorities (e.g. Turkey's application was slowed down by its problems with its Kurdish minority).
- New members agree to adopt and abide by all previous EU treaties and legislation with no opt outs (thus expected to join the Euro currency when they meet its entry criteria and may not opt out, unlike the UK).
- New member countries must adopt the principle of freedom of trade, health and safety regulations and apply explicit environmental standards.
- Member countries must be fundamentally democratic with free and fair elections, a record of upholding the rule of law and a functioning market economy. They should maintain (and have a record of) economic stability, with relatively low levels of unemployment, inflation and public debt.
- They must commit to a broad common foreign policy.

What is the Eurozone? Why is Britain not a member?
- The Eurozone is the group of countries that have adopted the euro as their currency.
- In 1997 Gordon Brown set five economic tests that had to be met before ministers would recommend the UK for euro entry and holding a referendum.
- His key test was whether the UK economy is coming together with those of countries in the Eurozone and whether this can be sustained in the long term (i.e. same stage of the economic cycle).
- The second test, linked to this, was whether sufficient flexibility existed to cope with economic change.
- The remaining three tests assessed the impact of joining the euro on jobs, foreign investment and the financial services industry.
- Since then there has been no stage at which the Prime Minister believed the tests had been met.
- Being outside the Eurozone cost many Britons dear in 2008 and 2009 as the exchange rate changed, making European holidays and goods much more expensive.
- However, in January 2009, Liberal Democrat leader Nick Clegg MP dismissed the idea that joining was essential, saying 'The euro is no magic wand'.

What benefits does Britain get on return for contributions to the EU budget?
- Inevitably the EU provides greater support to its poorer members, which results in countries such as France, Holland, Italy, Germany and the UK contributing more than is paid back in EU support.
- EU funds support agriculture, training and retraining, research and development for new technologies, major road and rail developments, flood prevention schemes and substantial amounts of investment both to combat global warming and to promote development in UK regions that are far from London.
- As living standards and incomes in poorer EU countries rise, so consumers' purchasing power in these countries rises, meaning that the UK can do well exporting to such countries.

Should the EU be involved in environmental policy-making such as the climate change debate?
- This is exactly the type of issue with which the EU is best equipped to deal.
- Before the dangers of global warming were understood, it was recognised that activities in one country could harm other countries – so Europe became concerned that nuclear power stations should be run safely after the Chernobyl power station disaster in Ukraine in 1986.

- The same concerns developed when it was realised that acid rain caused by pollution in eastern Europe could travel north and west to do great environmental damage in other countries such as the UK, Eire, Sweden and Finland.
- On environmental matters such as this, the problem is not limited to the boundaries of one country alone, which is why international decision-making, monitoring and co-operation are so important.
- On the issue of global warming, the less developed parts of the EU will need support and assistance in reducing the volume of carbon and methane they emit; they will need access to new technologies and support in switching from fossil fuels to clean or renewable forms of energy.
- If they are not helped to reduce carbon emissions, the consequences of their actions may not be felt in their own countries just as the burning of the Amazonian rainforest is thought to have caused, in part, extreme weather in southern parts of the USA (e.g. Hurricane Katrina), desertification in Africa, flooding in the UK and the melting of polar ice, with resultant rises in sea levels.
- On ethical and moral grounds alone, the EU needs to play its part in confronting this problem, which has the potential to change the planet for people living in every country and every continent.

Britain and the United Nations

Lesson objectives	Specification link: Unit 1, Theme 3
By the end of this spread the student should: • know about the membership of the United Nations • recognise the organisation and achievements of the United Nations • understand the UN Millennium Goals	

Focus

...on what each of the Millennium Development Goals involves, the progress on human rights over the 60 years of the UN's existence and why some people see the Security Council as preventing rather than promoting solutions to some of the world's most dangerous and pressing problems.

Key terms

• economic sanctions

• disarmament

• genocide

• refugees

• Security Council and veto

• UN Charter

Starter	If there were no UN and the world was as unequal as it is now, rich or powerful countries might see no need for change while poor countries could do little to improve their situation – just having a UN is an achievement in itself. See also UN activities and website in UK.
Development	Then focus on the Millennium Development Goals (MDGs), using the UN website or student research. Ask students in groups to focus on different Goals and then report back to the whole group with answers to questions such as: • What problems are MDGs trying to combat and where do they exist? • What needs to be done and how much progress is being made? Consider the work of the Security Council. This body has 15 members and any permanent member (UK, France, Russia, China, USA) can block a proposal even if everyone else agrees with it. So, if most countries want to get tough with North Korea, Russia or China may block action; on other issues France, the UK or USA may use a veto. The veto seems to paralyse decision-making and delay action. But it ensures that countries keep talking rather than go to war! Critics say that, if the Security Council intervened to prevent genocide more quickly, millions of people murdered in Africa (Rwanda, Sierra Leone, Darfur, DR Congo, Zimbabwe) might still be alive today. The UN General Assembly, with 192 member countries, receives reports and members speak and vote but it finds it difficult to take bold decisions. Emphasise the roles of the UN agencies, e.g. UNESCO, UNHRC and UNICEF. Distinguish between the International Court of Justice and the International Criminal Court (see p. 117, Student Book).

	Key achievements of the UN include peacekeeping, humanitarian aid, human rights, supporting refugees and tackling climate change.
Plenary	Go over the *Checklist* points. Students can work on the *Further issues* questions as research or homework. Or they could look more closely at UN work on climate change, refugees or human rights

Answers to questions in the Student Book

What's the issue?

Should the UN's main concern be humanitarian issues or peacekeeping?
Often the two are linked. Millions of people can be displaced by civil war or flooding or earthquakes. It would be artificial to focus on just one set of problems. But note the distinctions drawn on p119 of the Student Book about conflict prevention, peace-making, -keeping, -enforcement and -building.

What humanitarian issues face the UN in Africa? How effectively are they dealt with?
- Africa has great potential riches in terms of resources (gold, diamonds, oil, zinc, platinum, copper) but the wealth these assets could bring are not widely shared in the countries where they have been found.
- Boundaries of African countries (e.g. Zimbabwe) were often invented by colonial countries. Now loyalties and enmities of local people are sometimes exacerbated when there is not enough food or work for all, leading to civil war as one group seeks to gain the upper hand.
- Africa has been exploited over the years by those who wanted its resources – without appropriate payment being made.
- Many political regimes have been proved to be corrupt, from Uganda's Idi Amin in the 1970s to Zimbabwe's Robert Mugabe in the 2000s. Some have resorted to killing and murder on a scale that amounts to genocide.
- With global warming, the hottest areas of Africa are getting hotter, making it harder to grow food and find safe water (danger of disease), so more people want to move to more temperate climates.
- The humanitarian problems are of millions of refugees being moved around by civil wars and the changing climate; there is acute poverty, starvation, rural depopulation, disease, inequality and poor education.
- The African Union has been established in an attempt to help Africa overcome such problems but it often seems to act as a cosy club with procedures, reports and endless committees but member countries ready to tolerate even the worst excesses of their friends.

Is the UN truly representative of all member countries or is it too often influenced by the Great Powers like Britain, USA and China who are permanent members of the Security Council?
- The permanent members of the Security Council (with the power of veto) undoubtedly have great power and the ordinary members of the General Assembly have considerably less power.
- The rotating membership of the Security Council (i.e. ten other countries sit on the council on a rota basis) means little because they have no veto.
- Many suggestions have been made about how the position could be improved – including bringing in other nations as permanent members – e.g. Japan, India or Germany.
- Is it justifiable to have a veto at all? Why not allow the Security Council to make decisions by majority vote?
- Many commentators have suggested that one country should not be able to stand in the way of action favoured by the other fourteen members of the Security Council.

Margin questions

What arguments are there for and against the suggestion that the United Nations should have a democratically elected Parliamentary Assembly?
If all delegates to the UN were elected from their own countries, the General Assembly would become more like the European Parliament, with members from each country sitting in political parties and sometimes opposing each other. Just as Europe is sometimes accused of taking too much power or sovereignty away from member countries and their national governments, the same claims would no doubt be made of the UN. Once it became more representative and democratic, it would strive for more

powers and bigger budgets. This could be a step towards world government – but perhaps at present it is a step too far.

Review and research

Which of the Millennium Development Goals is the most important? Why do you think it is more important than the others?
This is a matter for debate. All are compelling. Perhaps groups of students could make the case for each and class members could vote on it.

Is enough publicity given to UN humanitarian work?
All the information is on the UN website (follow the links to peace-related activities). Some might think there is so much information that even the interested observer could be overloaded. Perhaps there is a case for more emphasis to be given to this part of the news than to the trivia about celebrities that dominates many popular newspapers and magazines.

What is the purpose and moral justification for the International Court of Justice (ICJ) in The Hague?
The Court is the principal judicial body associated with the United Nations. It was established by the UN Charter in 1945 and began work in 1946 in the Peace Palace, The Hague (Netherlands). The Court has 15 judges. In accordance with international law, it settles legal disputes between states and gives advisory opinions on legal matters referred to it by agencies and other bodies within the UN. In contentious cases, the ICJ produces a binding ruling between states that agree to submit to the ruling of the Court, and thus it provides an alternative to going to war, or may resolve an existing conflict. The Court does not have the power to impose a ruling if a state is unwilling to co-operate or treat its judgment as binding. Many people believe that rogue states and their leaders should be subject to international law, especially in cases of genocide – matters such as these are dealt with by the International Criminal Court, a totally separate body.
NB: The ICJ has no jurisdiction to try individuals accused of war crimes or crimes against humanity. It is not a criminal court and does not have a prosecutor able to initiate proceedings. This task is undertaken by:
- national courts
- the criminal tribunals established by the United Nations (such as the International Criminal Tribunal for the former Yugoslavia (ICTY)
- the **International Criminal Court**, set up under the Rome Statute.

CITIZENSHIP STUS

Britain and the Commonwealth of Nations

Lesson objectives	Specification link: Unit 1, Theme 3
By the end of this spread the student should: • know about the membership of the Commonwealth of Nations • understand the role and importance of the Commonwealth of Nations • recognise the achievements of the Commonwealth of Nations	

Focus

...on what Commonwealth nations have in common – they are mostly former British colonies so they often maintain English language as one, if not the only, official language and they generally maintain their friendship with Britain and retain some elements of the British systems of democracy and rule of law.

Key terms

- British Empire
- colonies
- Commonwealth Games
- democracy

- Harare Declaration 1991
- non-governmental organizations (NGOs)
- racism
- sovereign country

Linked activity sheets

- The Commonwealth of Nations and the European Union

Starter	Use the map on p. 114 of the Student Book to identify some of the countries that belong to the Commonwealth. Make sure your students can identify one or two Commonwealth countries in each of the six inhabited continents.
Development	Start off by emphasising the difference between the Commonwealth and the EU – it doesn't make laws, it doesn't have a parliament – but it does help its members to work co-operatively, getting to know each other and helping each other out. It sometimes tries to help as an 'honest broker' if tension and conflict exist within or between member countries. With its worldwide membership it is also well placed to promote the UN Millennium Development Goals. It gives high priority to encouraging sustainable 'green' projects. Because the Commonwealth is sometimes seen as being less political than bodies such as the EU, it is trusted by its members and others. The Commonwealth gives a high priority to encouraging trade between countries and to finding opportunities for developing countries to sell their goods in the markets of developed countries. Because most members have had close links to the UK in the past, the Commonwealth is a powerful instrument for spreading British ideas and culture as well as our respect for democratic principles,

	human rights and the rule of law.
Plenary	Go over the *Checklist* points. Students can work on the *Further issues* questions as research or homework. Or they could research the ways in which the Commonwealth monitors elections in member countries.

Answers to questions in the Student Book

What's the issue?

What is the point of taking a 'symbolic move' which cannot be effectively enforced?

- Suspending Zimbabwe from Commonwealth membership effectively signalled to the rest of the world that Zimbabwe had broken the rules.
- This was a powerful way of emphasising that the remaining 53 members of the Commonwealth take democracy seriously.
- Other countries that have had their membership suspended at different times include Fiji, Nigeria and Pakistan.

Do Commonwealth leaders have a moral right to condemn a sovereign country?

- Membership of the Commonwealth is entirely voluntary and is open to countries with a clear link to an existing member and which share the ideals of other Commonwealth members.
- If members do not keep the rules, that is their business and as sovereign countries they can do as they please.
- As leaders of countries committed to democracy, those attending Commonwealth meetings cannot intervene in the affairs of other countries, but if a country's behaviour falls below the standards required by the organisation, members have the right to say so.
- Morality is a matter of right or wrong and being true to one's principles, so no Commonwealth country can ignore misbehaviour by fellow members.

Does membership of the EU create conflict with membership of the Commonwealth?

- In the days of the British Empire the principle of 'imperial preference' sometimes operated in which in some, but not all commodities, free trade applied – i.e. no tariffs were levied.
- If the UK had not become part of the EU and the new European Single Market, a Commonwealth 'free trade area' might have been established.
- In reality, trade is best organised between countries between whom trade is advantageous.
- There are, for example, much more obvious trade partners for Australia and New Zealand than other Commonwealth countries on the other side of the world

What is ironic about the reference to the Harare Declaration?

Harare is capital of Zimbabwe. In the 1991 Harare Declaration, Commonwealth leaders stated their commitment to:

- the principles of international peace and order, global economic development and the rule of international law
- the liberty of the individual under the law, equal rights for all citizens regardless of gender, race, colour, creed or political belief, and the individual's inalienable right to participate by means of free and democratic political processes framing the society in which he or she lives
- oppose racial discrimination as an unmitigated evil, racial prejudice and intolerance being a dangerous sickness and a threat to the healthy development of a country
- oppose all forms of racial oppression, and to remain true to the principles of human dignity and equality
- the importance and urgency of economic and social development to satisfy the basic needs and aspirations of the vast majority of the peoples of the world, and seek the progressive removal of the wide disparities in living standards amongst our members.

The irony comes from the fact that Robert Mugabe's regime broke most of, if not all, these very commitments that had been made in its own capital city.

Margin questions

Which former British colonies have resigned from or not joined the Commonwealth of Nations – and why?

- Burma (Myanmar) and Yemen are former colonies that chose not to join the Commonwealth on gaining independence. Other countries that declined Commonwealth membership were mainly in the Middle

East, including Egypt, Iraq, Palestine (now largely the state of Israel), Sudan, Kuwait, Bahrain, Oman, Qatar, and the United Arab Emirates. The Republic of Ireland left the Commonwealth upon becoming a republic in 1949.
- Britian treated most clolonial peoples very poorly.

How important are the Commonwealth Games? Why are they called the Friendly Games?

- The Commonwealth Games is a unique, world class, multi-sports event held once every 4 years and is often referred to as the 'Friendly Games' because the atmosphere seems like a family celebrating – people meeting again who haven't seen each other for a while.
- To improve society and the general well-being of the people of the Commonwealth, the CGF also encourages and assists education via sport development and physical recreation, with the aim of promoting values that inspire and unite Commonwealth citizens, celebrating humanity, equality and destiny.
- The 2010 Commonwealth Games are to be held in Delhi and in 2014 the Games return to the UK, to be held in Glasgow.

Review and research

What features must be present for a place to be described as a sovereign country?

If sovereignty is the exclusive right to exercise, within a particular area of territory, the functions of a nation-state without being answerable to a higher authority, it is clear that most former Commonwealth members previously had to recognise the rights of the British government to dictate how their country was run. Now such countries are independent, they are sovereign countries in their own right. They may choose to agree to Commonwealth policies or initiatives but they don't have to and no one can make them.

In 1949 the British Commonwealth became the 'Commonwealth of Nations'. Why was the original name changed? How significant was it?

Although most of the countries belonging to the Commonwealth have a past connection to Britain, the existence of 'British' in the title could have been seen by some as a continuance of Britain's role as colonial master, as in the days of Empire. By removing 'British' from the title, the Commonwealth asserts its existence as a free and voluntary association of equal and democratic states.

Should the Commonwealth have a military peace-keeping force?

Although the Commonwealth urges good behaviour and adherence to agreed principles on all its members, it does not have a strong executive branch to carry out complicated and demanding peace-keeping operations. It is difficult to see how the development of such a role could do more than duplicate existing peace-keeping operations conducted under the aegis of the United Nations (UN) or the North Atlantic Treaty Organisation (NATO).

For reference

The Commonwealth comprises 53 of the world's countries, across 6 inhabited continents. The combined population is 2.1 billion people, of which about half live in India. There is only one member of the present Commonwealth that has never had any constitutional link to the British Empire or a Commonwealth member: Mozambique, a former Portuguese colony, was admitted in 1995. A full list of members is:

Antigua and Barbuda	Ghana	Namibia	Solomon Islands
Australia	Grenada	Nauru	South Africa
The Bahamas	Guyana	New Zealand	Sri Lanka
Bangladesh	India	Nigeria	Swaziland
Barbados	Jamaica	Pakistan	Tanzania
Belize	Kenya	Papua New Guinea	Tonga
Botswana	Kiribati	Saint Kitts and Nevis	Trinidad and Tobago
Brunei	Lesotho	Saint Lucia	Tuvalu
Cameroon	Malawi	Saint Vincent and	Uganda
Canada	Malaysia	the Grenadines	United Kingdom
Cyprus	Maldives	Samoa	Vanuatu
Dominica	Malta	Seychelles	Zambia
Fiji (suspended)	Mauritius	Sierra Leone	
The Gambia	Mozambique	Singapore	

Global citizenship:
The strength of disagreements

Lesson objectives	Specification link: Unit 1, Theme 3
By the end of this spread the student should: • know about International Humanitarian Law • recognise ways in which international law can be enforced • understand the disagreements over human rights and equality	

Focus

...on how, if wars are really unavoidable, harm to children, civilians and the elderly can be limited. Also focus on efforts to reduce the most cruel weapons of war and how military personnel who are wounded or taken prisoner should be treated with respect – and possible consequences for war leaders if they do not keep to such rules.

Key terms

• Amnesty International

• Geneva Convention

• genocide & Genocide Convention 1948

• ICRC - International Committee of the Red Cross

• International Criminal Court (ICC)

• International Humanitarian Law (IHL)

• UN Human Rights Commissioner

Linked activity sheets

• War criminals

Starter	Start off with exploding bullets, biological or chemical weapons – why do countries at war respect rules not to use such weapons? Because they don't want their armed forces to suffer the dreadful injuries they can cause any more than the other side does.
Development	Are any other weapons banned from the battlefield? Princess Diana campaigned successfully against the use of land mines, which can completely shatter people's bodies – with a ban taking effect in 1997 (though millions of mines still need to be deactivated). Although not banned, great efforts are made to limit the use of nuclear weapons and the numbers of countries – particularly unstable ones such as Iraq and North Korea - that have access to them. IHL requires combatants to avoid harming civilians wherever possible. In the 2009 Gaza war, ICRC found evidence of medical treatment being denied to wounded civilians and Human Rights Commissioner Navi Pillay described shelling a building in which civilians were sheltering for safety, and the resulting deaths, as 'elements of what would constitute war crimes'.

CITIZENSHIP STUDIES

	After the Second World War, many German leaders were tried at Nuremburg and executed for war crimes. Such trials are now conducted by special tribunals established by the UN or by the ICC, though they no longer impose death sentences. Amnesty International highlights whippings, torture, death sentences and official cruelty in other countries.
Plenary	Go over the *Checklist* points. Students can work on the *Further issues* questions as research or homework. Or they could research the progress of cases at the ICC or at the International Criminal Tribunal for former Yugoslavia (ICTY), where Radovan Karadzic is being tried.

Answers to questions in the Student Book

What's the issue?

Why is International Humanitarian Law (IHL) needed?
- War is brutal and in many cases barbaric.
- Since 1864 serious attempts have been made to establish ground rules that protect children, civilians, the elderly and military personnel who surrender or who can no longer fight.
- IHL aims to ensure prisoners of war are kept safe and treated with dignity.
- Genocide is now a recognised crime and killing a large number of people because of who they are (as the Serbs killed 8,000 Bosnian men and boys in Srebrenica in 1995) can lead to the leaders responsible appearing in court and serving long periods in prison if found guilty.
- IHL tries to prevent particularly cruel weapons, such as biological or chemical warfare, from being used.

How does the International Committee of the Red Cross (ICRC) make a difference?
- The ICRC is a non-governmental sovereign entity.
- Its legal status comes from the four Geneva Conventions of 1949, as well as its own rules.
- Its official mission statement says it 'is an impartial, neutral, and independent organization whose exclusively humanitarian mission is to protect the lives and dignity of victims of war and internal violence and to provide them with assistance'.
- ICRC's main tasks are to monitor compliance of warring parties with the Geneva Conventions so as
- to organise nursing and care for those who are wounded on the battlefield
- to supervise the treatment of prisoners of war and make confidential interventions with detaining authorities
- to help with the search for missing persons in an armed conflict (tracing service)
- to organise protection and care for civil populations
- to act as a neutral intermediary between warring parties

- In 1965 the ICRC adopted the principles of: humanity, impartiality, neutrality, independence, volunteerism, unity, and universality.
- In 2009 the ICRC played a key part in getting humanitarian aid to refugees displaced by fighting in Gaza, Pakistan and Sri Lanka.

Why is IHL more difficult to enforce than other kinds of law?
- In every country there are specific laws outlining particular offences, a police service to catch people who break these laws and courts established to deal with the alleged offenders.
- Such clarity and certainty is often absent when it comes to IHL.
- Keeping track of what happens during a military engagement isn't easy: witnesses may have a one-sided view of events and there is no police force to make arrests, so arrests occur long after the event, if at all.
- Often military leaders will try to defend themselves, saying they were 'only obeying orders'.
- The law itself is much more a set of principles than the detailed rules on which cases in domestic cases are often based.
- Trials and court hearings may take place thousands of miles from where the initial offences were committed and often many years later – by which time memories may have faded to some extent.

CITIZENSHIP STUDIES

Review and research

Are wars caused mainly by economics, politics or geography?

Many wars have been caused over history by the desire of one ruler or country to control the territory of another. This may be because the one country has little land of its own or it may covet the resources that go with the land of another – which may have a coastline, oil or other valuable commodities such as coal or platinum or copper. Conflicts may arise between tribes or different ethnic groups or different religions that enjoy scarce resources – the wars in the former Yugoslavia and between Israel and her Arab neighbours come into this category. Many wars are about which nation will be able to rule over a larger territory than it holds at present – this is about dominance and involves all three of economics, politics and geography.

Are children, the elderly and the wounded adequately protected by IHL?

- Children, the elderly and the wounded still get hurt and their lives are disrupted by war.
- IHL offers some attempt to minimise such harm.
- As a result, things are better than they would be if IHL did not exist.
- While there are many innocent victims of war, millions of refugees are provided with rudimentary shelter, food and healthcare by ICRC and the limitation on some of the most terrible potential weapons of war to some extent reduces levels of death and injury.
- As IHL becomes more established and more combatant, leaders find themselves being tried before special tribunals or the ICC, and the potential consequences for them personally of even fighting and winning a war might make them think twice before launching their attacks.

Should it be just as much a criminal offence to injure someone in wartime as peacetime?

- Many people engaged in fighting would say they were defending themselves or their neighbours or that they were ordered to fight by their superiors.
- Criminal offences are part of the rule of law, yet often there seems to be very little sign of law as people shoot or bomb each other in wartime.
- If every member of the armed forces who killed or injured someone in wartime had to be tried in court for assault, manslaughter or murder, would this make war more or less likely?
- Perhaps criminal charges should be restricted to those who give the orders – politicians and military leaders?
- This is something to debate in class.

Why might countries such as China, Russia, India and the USA choose not to join the ICC?

- When the ICC was established in 2002 as a permanent criminal court to investigate and prosecute genocide, crimes against humanity, and war crimes, President George W Bush's administration in the USA made clear its intention never to join it.
- Since President Obama has taken office, Secretary of State Clinton has indicated that the US will end its 'hostility' towards the Court.
- But by June 2009 the Obama Administration had made no formal policy decision on the ICC.
- Russia, Israel, Sudan and the USA signed the Rome Statute that brought the ICC into existence but have since failed to ratify it.
- Those who failed even to sign up to the ICC (including China and India) have claimed that, since the court acts only where there is no functioning legal system in the country where genocide or other crimes occur, it cannot apply to them because they do have functioning court systems that afford protection to witnesses, victims and defendants alike.
- But many believe that leaders of the non-signing/non-ratifying countries feared that they themselves could be arrested and taken to the ICC for trial for wrongdoing initiated by them and that, if their own country had signed up to support the court, it would be more difficult to resist such trials.
- Claims have also been made that the ICC does not fit easily into a constitutional structure and that judges and prosecutors may behave in an arbitrary manner, picking and choosing between those they wish to prosecute.
- The answer, say the non-signers and non-ratifiers, is to appoint special tribunals (to cover the situation in former Yugoslavia or Sierra Leone) as and when it is appropriate to do so.

A force for good

Lesson objectives	Specification link: Unit 1, Theme 3
By the end of this spread the student should: • understand the effectiveness of UK action through the UN and other bodies in undertaking debt relief and peacekeeping • recognise the need for humanitarian aid and how it is provided	

Focus

...on the UK's role in the world – leading the pressure to cancel the debts of poor countries, helping out with peacekeeping and providing aid and advice through DFID, contributing humanitarian relief when crises occur and encouraging free and fair trade with developing countries.

Key terms

• conflict prevention

• peacemaking – peacekeeping – peace enforcement – peacebuilding

• Department for Internal Development (DFID)

• heavily indebted poor countries (HIPCs)

• humanitarian aid

• International Monetary Fund (IMF)

• UN Central Emergency Response Fund (CERF)

• United Nations High Commissioner for Refugees (UNHCR)

• World Bank

Linked activity sheets

• The poverty cycle

• Wants and needs

• Peace one day

• Development indicators

Starter	Look at the four examples on p. 119 when crises meant other countries desperately urgently needed aid. What aid would they need? Why could the people not provide it for themselves?
Development	When there is serious flooding or earthquakes, people may lose their home, food, clothes and may be injured.
	These problems also arose during the 2004 tsunami as well as the Zimbabwe harvest failures of 2007 and 2008.
	The US found it difficult to cope when hit by Hurricane Katrina, so what chance would poor people in developing countries have?
	Ask students to research/understand the work of the UN High Commissioner for Refugees (UNHCR) and the support systems it organises.
	Don't forget to emphasise the important role played by the UN, the work of French doctors through Médecins Sans Frontières and also by non-governmental voluntary organisations such as Oxfam, the Red Cross and Christian Aid.
	Britain does more than provide aid and encourage trade – we get

	involved in the peace agenda – everything from conflict prevention to peacebuilding. Make sure students understand the five different stages listed on p. 119. Then focus on the debt relief programme for heavily indebted poor countries, which the UK pioneered at the G7 Summit in 2000 – 35 countries have benefitted, allowing them to meet their priority needs – e.g. improving water supplies, education, healthcare and their rural infrastructures.
Plenary	Go over the *Checklist* points. Students can work on the *Further issues* questions as research or homework. Or they could look at the DFID website to understand the many ways in which the UK provides positive support to countries in the less developed world.

Answers to questions in the Student Book

What's the issue?

Why can developing countries not solve their own problems?
- In the UK, thanks to the welfare state, most of the poorest citizens have better health, homes, food and healthcare than many people in developing countries.
- Many developing countries still look like traditional societies, in some areas at least, without major road, rail, telephone, employment, education, electricity, housing and healthcare infrastructures.
- Often such countries are divided societies with a few very rich, well educated, privileged people and most others being poor and barely educated, totally dependent on jobs if they can find them.
- Developing countries are often rich in resources such as oil, coal, platinum and copper but they depend on others to exploit these – and the less developed country may not receive a fair return.
- Often the leaders of these countries have borrowed large sums in the past supposedly to create a better infrastructure of modern industries but in many cases the money was frittered away on building grand palaces for the leaders, for which the country has to pay vast amounts of interest.
- As much as 50% of income earned from selling goods overseas may be taken just to pay off interest on borrowing from other countries without reducing the basic debt at all.
- That is why the UK led a campaign at G7 meetings to cancel the debts of less developed countries so they could spend more on relieving poverty and improving the country's education, healthcare and basic infrastructures.

Why should rich countries give aid or cancel debts to developing countries?
- Given our privileged position as the fourth richest country in the world, it would show extreme selfishness and moral weakness if we were unwilling to help those with fewer resources.
- Once developing countries have established basic services and industries, they are more likely to trade with the UK, buying from us as well as selling to us. That way, everyone benefits.

Why have debt reduction programmes made less progress than was generally hoped?
- In 2008, the International Monetary Fund (IMF) reported on the HIPC Initiative, which is a comprehensive approach to debt reduction for heavily indebted poor countries.
- Up to 2008, debt reduction packages had been approved for 35 countries, 29 of them in Africa, providing US$51 billion in debt-service relief over time; 6 additional countries were also eligible for HIPC Initiative assistance.
- Although the largest creditors (the World Bank, the African Development Bank, the IMF, the Inter-American Development Bank, and all Paris Club creditors) have provided debt relief as promised and in line with their commitments, others are lagging behind.
- Smaller institutions, including some commercial creditors, (accounting for about 25% of total HIPC Initiative costs) have delivered only a small share of their expected relief so far.
- For example, relief given to date by commercial creditors is still at barely 40% of the sums promised.
- As an added complication, some commercial creditors have initiated legal cases against HIPCs for various reasons, making the whole debt-reduction process all the more difficult.

Review and research

CITIZENSHIP STUDIES

Why have debt reduction programmes not fully lived up to the hopes of those who established them?

See above. Given that the HIPC debt-relief scheme is voluntary, the IMF and the World Bank say they will continue to use moral pressure to encourage creditors to participate in the initiative and to deliver fully their share of HIPC Initiative debt relief.

How much do UN peace-related activities contribute in reality to world stability?

- A small-scale dispute can quickly grow and get out of hand.
- That is why (i) conflict prevention strategies to try to prevent a dispute turning into a violent conflict are particularly important. If a conflict does break out, the UN enters into (ii) peacemaking to try to get both sides to negotiate – to resolve their differences by negotiation rather than killing. (iii) Peace enforcement involves taking active steps to restore international peace and security. Once the fighting has stopped, (iv) peacekeeping is critical to stop the dispute starting again.
- The fifth of these processes is (v) peacebuilding, trying to keep an agreement going and getting the country back to normal.
- Many conflicts take steps (ii), (iii) and (iv) in a different order, lurching backwards and forwards as the dispute adapts and changes.
- Some of the disputes with which the UN gets involved might resolve themselves without its support – but many might not and could escalate into a much bigger regional conflict or world war.
- In March 2009 the UN had 92,000 uniformed and 18,000 civilian personnel from 117 countries working in 16 conflicts – the estimated cost for such activities during the 2008/9 year was $7.1 billion.

Does the UN need more powers to intervene directly in the affairs of countries – such as Zimbabwe – which behave badly? How could reform of the UN Security Council help?

- It could be argued that the UN already has the powers but, because of the veto in the Security Council, rarely uses them.
- If the Security Council went over to majority voting, or a similar system where one veto did not bring a project to a rapid halt, the UN could adopt a more proactive or interventionist approach to world problems.
- See also Teacher notes for *Theme 3, Spread 11*.

CITIZENSHIP STUDIES

A call to conscience

Lesson objectives	Specification link: Unit 1, Theme 3
By the end of this spread the student should: • understand the challenges facing the UN, EU and global community • recognise the relationship between MEDCs and LEDCs in terms of trade and aid	

Focus

...on life expectancy – this largely reflects the quality of life in different countries (and therefore compares living standards between them). In the UK life expectancy at birth is nearly 79 years (more for women than men) but a person born in Ukraine could expect to live for 10 fewer years and someone from Ghana for 20 fewer years. Life expectancy in South Africa is below 49 years.

Key terms

• division of labour
• employees
• G7 and G20 countries
• LEDCs and MEDCs

• life expectancy
• multinational companies
• tariffs
• World Trade Organization (WTO)

Linked activity sheets

• The poverty cycle
• Wants and needs

Starter	Why is the life expectancy of a newborn baby born in an EU country 11 years greater than the world average?
Development	Life expectancy tables provide a good indication of relative standards of living, reflecting income and wealth. Such tables often reflect the extent to which civil wars or other disturbances occur, how many refugees have to be catered for, whether clean water is available for all and how much of a problem HIV/AIDS is in the country. On p121, the Student Book draws attention to the lack of education and training in many developing countries resulting in people adopting a generalist approach to work rather than (e.g. in building a house) each person having particular skills – architect, electrician, plumber, carpenter/joiner, etc. There is also the issue of population – only 3 of the world's 20 countries with the highest populations are members of the G7. Many of these countries form the G20 group of emerging economies. There would be big advantages if these poorer countries could be developed (via trade and/or aid) so there was greater equality in living standards throughout the world. Such a development should mean greater interdependence and more trade between countries – reducing the possibility of future conflicts – particularly if the WTO could persuade developed countries to help developing countries to expand trade and reduce tariffs.

	Consider the advantages and disadvantages of multinational companies such as BP, Shell, Nike, Microsoft. They locate as much of their business as they can in low-cost countries and sell goods elsewhere at the highest prices possible. They provide jobs in poorer countries but such countries rarely benefit from the big profits they make.
Plenary	Go over the *Checklist* points. Students can work on the *Further issues* questions as research or homework. They could look at life expectancy at birth figures for different areas and consider reasons for differences.

Answers to questions in the Student Book

What's the issue?

Why is life expectancy higher in G7 countries?

- The G7 countries (Japan, Canada, France, Italy, Germany, UK and USA) are the wealthiest countries in the world with the highest standards of living – and this is reflected in their life expectancy.
- People have access to water and good food, high quality education and health services, mostly comfortable homes and a largely pollution-free atmosphere to sustain above-average levels of income and wealth.
- All the countries have extensive provisions for those on low incomes at least to provide a 'safety net'.

Why is life expectancy in the EU different from the world average?

- The same factors explain why average life expectancy in the EU (77 years) is higher than the world average (66 years).
- Even within an individual country, life expectancy in some areas at birth will be much higher than in others: there is said to be a gap of 14 years between life expectancy rates in the most and least prosperous areas of Sheffield.
- The wealthier EU countries such as France, Italy, Germany, Ireland and the UK are above the average EU life expectancy at birth while less well off countries that have joined the EU more recently at present have lower life expectancy at birth, e.g. Slovenia, Slovakia, Czech Republic, Poland, Latvia and Estonia. As their prosperity levels rise, their life expectancy rates at birth are likely to do the same.
- The world average is lower than the EU average because, although there are a few non-European countries with averages well above that of the EU (e.g. Japan, Australia and Canada), there are many that are far below the EU and world averages (e.g. Russia, Bangladesh, Kenya and South Africa).
- A factor that makes a big difference in Africa is the very high incidence of HIV/AIDS.

What do many of the countries with life expectancy below the world average have in common?

- Countries below the world average include Russia, Pakistan, Bangladesh, Ghana, Kenya, DR Congo, South Africa, Zimbabwe, Afghanistan, Sierra Leone and Swaziland.
- They are poor countries with low levels of income and education, where many people cannot afford to access health care.
- People in some of these countries have difficulty in accessing clean water and in some of them cholera has at times been a real problem. Many of them have a big problem with HIV/AIDS.
- Many have had civil wars or have been involved in regional disputes, resulting in large numbers of refugees living in camps, with limited opportunity to earn a living and maintain a good standard of living.

Margin questions

In the UK a house might be built by different groups of workers each specialising in a trade – e.g. architects, foundation workers, bricklayers, plumbers, carpenters/joiners, electricians, painters/decorators and landscapers. How might a house be built in an LEDC?

In many LEDCs there is less education and training, so more workers are generalists whereas in the UK workers often tend to specialise in particular skills. Having the same person build the walls and organise the carpentry is less likely to achieve a high quality finish compared to the result likely to be achieved when division of labour operates and each stage is handled by an appropriate specialist.

CITIZENSHIP STUDIES

Review and research

What steps could a country take to increase the life expectancy of its population?

Looking at life expectancy at birth tables over a number of years reveals that better off people are healthier people who live longer. As income and employment levels in a country rise, so they can afford to improve education and healthcare, live in better houses, reduce pollution, perhaps work fewer hours per week and enjoy the benefits of clean air and a clean water supply. The better the healthcare in an area, the more likely that diseases such as malaria, tuberculosis or HIV/AIDS will be successfully treated and screening facilities to identify possible cancer, heart or other complex health problems will be readily available to all.

Why might a high level of life expectancy be seen as a disadvantage?

High levels of life expectancy are good for individuals – showing they are healthy. But as people get older, pension funds need to pay pensions for longer. This is causing problems in some advanced economies because, at the very time when the birth rate is falling, the number of people expecting to receive a pension is rising much more quickly. With these population characteristics, the working population is called upon to earn enough to provide pensions for the increasing numbers of retired people.

Do multinational companies help developing countries in the long run?

- Many multinational companies do provide much employment in developing countries – often they set up a manufacturing base in such countries or else call centres to deal with orders and queries from customers.
- But the companies will then aim to sell the goods and services they produce in other countries where incomes are high enough for high prices to be charged.
- Multinational companies organise their activities all over the world in ways that guarantee they maximise the profits they make – but the developing country is unlikely to gain much benefit from such profits.
- As developing countries prosper, the employees' incomes will rise and it is at this stage that multinational companies go out of their way to offer products for the newly better-off workers to buy.

Introduction to Unit 2

Examiner's advice

Unit 2, participation in society, is a controlled assessment unit which is taken by everyone following the Short Course GCSE. (Those taking the Full Course GCSE will also take the Unit 4 controlled assessment.) Unit 2 requires students to undertake an enquiry into a Citizenship issue that matters to them.

Key features

To begin with, students must choose an issue which will be the basis of their enquiry. The issue must be based on one of the nine range and topic areas which form the basis of the Edexcel GCSE Citizenship Studies specification.

The nine range and topic areas are:

- Political, legal and human rights and freedoms.
- Civil and criminal law and the justice system. (This can bring in areas such as the police, courts, prison and other punishments.)
- Democratic and electoral processes (voting systems) and parliamentary democracy.
- How different kinds of rights and freedoms developed both in the UK and abroad.
- The operation, role and importance of the media.
- Policies and practices that support sustainable development.
- Links between the economy and citizenship and the relationship between employers and the employed.
- Why the UK is becoming a more diverse and changing society.
- A global dimension: the European Union, the Commonwealth and the United Nations.

The four essential requirements of Unit 2 are that students must show their ability to:

- Enquire into a citizenship issue.
- Evaluate different ideas and viewpoints, presenting a convincing argument.
- Participate in action to address the chosen citizenship issue.
- Evaluate the impact of their own actions.

Students will need help and advice on some key tasks which will be important to their enquiry. These are most likely to be:

- Making an informed choice about the issue which will form the basis of students' enquiry (which must be from a different range and content area than the one used for Unit 4 if you are doing the Full Course GCSE).
- Whether to work as an individual or as part of a group.
- Planning the amount of time students can allocate to Unit 2 in relation to the other subjects that they are studying.
- What sort of resources students will need to make the enquiry a success.
- The sort of methods that students can use in their issue and action and how these can be tested.
- How to gather, use and evaluate evidence to support their enquiry.
- The skills involved in using the skills of advocacy and representation in your enquiry.
- How to evaluate the strengths, weaknesses and overall level of success of the enquiry.

How Unit 2 will be assessed

There are 50 marks in total for the Unit 2 assessment. The 50 marks are split into four main assessment areas:

- Enquiry (10 marks).

- Application of skills of advocacy and representation (15 marks).

- Participation in action (15 marks).

- Evaluation (10 marks).

- Unit 2 contributes 60% to the Short Course GCSE grade and 30% to the Full Course GCSE grade.

- Because it is a Controlled Assessment, the writing up of the participation issue has to take place in sessions supervised by teachers.

- A response form for the writing up of the participation issue report will be provided by Edexcel and will form a guide to the four assessment areas listed above.

- Students will have a total of 3 hours to complete the report but this will usually be split into smaller blocks of time.

- Students will not be allowed to take their work home once the 'writing up' starts. It has to be stored securely in your school or college.

- Students' participation issue reports will be marked first by their Citizenship teachers (internal assessment), and then a sample of the work from your school/college will be marked by an independent assessor appointed by Edexcel (external assessment).

The Student Book provides a step-by-step approach to the controlled assessment, with examiner comments, examples, clarification of terms and hints on how to relate these to the contexts students have chosen. These, in conjunction with the Teacher Support Material from Edexcel, will support you throughout the controlled assessment task.